Demystifying
ISO 9001:2000

ISBN 0-13-062046-7

90000

9 790130 620469

Demystifying
ISO 9001:2000

Gerard W. Paradis
John R. Trubiano

Prentice Hall PTR
Upper Saddle River, NJ 07458
www.phptr.com

Library of Congress Cataloging-in-Publication Data

Paradis, Gerard W.,
  Demystifying ISO 9001:2000 / Gerard W. Paradis, John R. Trubiano.— 2nd ed.
    p. cm.
  ISBN 0-13-062046-7
    1. ISO 9000 Series Standards. I. Trubiano, John R. II. Title.

TS156.6 .P375 2002
658.5'62—dc21   2001036524

Editorial/Production Supervision: *Vincent Janoski*
Acquisitions Editor: *Bernard Goodwin*
Editorial Assistant: *Michelle Vincente*
Marketing Manager: *Dan DePasquale*
Manufacturing Buyer: *Alexis Heydt*
Cover Design: *Talar Boorujy*
Cover Design Director: *Jerry Votta*

© 2002 by Prentice Hall
Published by Prentice Hall PTR
Prentice-Hall, Inc.
Upper Saddle River, NJ 07458

Information
Mapping·

Prentice Hall books are widely used by corporations and government agencies for training, marketing, and resale. The publisher offers discounts on this book when ordered in bulk quantities. For more information, contact Corporate Sales Department, phone: 800-382-3419; fax: 201-236-7141; email: corpsales@ prenhall.com; or write Corporate Sales Department, Prentice Hall PTR, One Lake Street, Upper Saddle River, NJ 07458.

All products or services mentioned in this book are the trademarks or service marks of their respective companies or organizations.

This manual has been developed using the standards of the Information Mapping methodology. Information Mapping is a registered service mark of Information Mapping, Inc. Info-Map is a registered trademark of Information Mapping, Inc.

Printed in the United States of America

10 9 8 7 6 5 4 3 2 1

ISBN 0-13-062046-7

Pearson Education LTD
Pearson Education Australia PTY, Limited
Pearson Education Singapore, Pte. Ltd.
Pearson Education North Asia Ltd.
Pearson Education Canada, Ltd.
Pearson Education de Mexico, S.A. de C.V.
Pearson Education-Japan
Pearson Education Malaysia, Pte. Ltd.
Pearson Education, Upper Saddle River, New Jersey

Contents

Chapter 6—Resource Management

Chapter 7—Product Realization

Overview

Introduction | *Demystifying ISO 9001:2000* is the follow-up guide to the 1994 edition of *Demystifying ISO 9000*.

Description | The purpose of this book is to provide readers with a basic, accessible and easy-to-understand guide that will assist them in attaining ISO 9001:2000 compliance.

Chapters 1–3 | Chapters 1, 2, and 3 provide

- a recommended approach to implementing Quality Management System requirements needed to achieve certification
- comparisons between the 2000 version and the 1994 edition, and
- definition of Quality Management Systems.

Chapters 4–8 | Chapters 4, 5, 6, 7 and 8 provide the details of each of the five (5) major sections and related topics.

The table below describes the primary subjects covered for each section of ISO 9001:2000.

Subject	Description
Requirement	The primary requirements called for in this section of the ISO 9001:2000 Standard.
What this means	Further clarification of the requirements.
Evidence	Specific information requirements that verify conformance for this section of the Standard.
Auditor questions ?	Typical questions an auditor might ask for this section.

Continued on next page

Overview, Continued

Chapters 4–8
(continued)

Note: In addition, each section and/or topic has other related and pertinent information to help in the understanding of the requirements.

Sections 0–3

The ISO 9001:2000 sections 0, 1, 2, and 3 below are described on pages 1 through 4.

- Section 0 - Introduction
- Section 1 - Scope
- Section 2 - Normative Reference, and
- Section 3 - Terms and Definitions.

Chapter 9

Chapter 9 highlights the ***new points emphasis*** in the Standard and advises readers on ***things to consider*** when planning the transitioning from the 1994 version to the new ISO 9001:2000 Standard.

Preface

Introduction

In March of 1993, Team ISO of Information Mapping, Inc. published the first edition of *Demystifying ISO 9000: Information Mapping's Guide to the ISO 9000 Standards*. The book's aim was to help readers better understand the five basic ISO 9000 Standards. It was also meant to provide a proven path-forward to certification to one of the three ISO 9000 Quality System Models (ISO 9001, 9002, or 9003).

The response to the guide was overwhelmingly positive. *Demystifying ISO 9000: Information Mapping's Guide to the ISO 9000 Standards* became an instant bestseller, and the reviews raved about the usability of the text. Over 50 organizations purchased multiple copies and distributed them to their ISO coordination teams.

The 2000 version

The 2000 version of *Demystifying ISO 9001:2000 Information Mapping's Guide to the ISO 9000 Standards* was created to respond to customer demands and to parallel the revisions to the ISO 9000 Standards published on December 15, 2000.

In addition to covering the changes in the Standard, this guide has been totally revised and includes chapters or sections on

- The ISO 9000 Standards
- The Certification Process
- Comparing ISO 9001:2000 and ISO 9001:1994
- Documentation and Records Requirements
- What Is a Quality Management System?
- Quality Management Principles
- Quality Management System Requirements
- Management Responsibility Requirements
- Resource Management Requirements
- Product Realization Requirements
- Measurement, Analysis, and Improvement Requirements, and
- Transition Planning for ISO 9001:2000.

Continued on next page

Information Mapping and ISO

The idea for using the principles of Information Mapping to document quality systems for conformance to the ISO 9000 Standards evolved from a series of seminars held by Information Mapping, Inc. for quality assurance personnel at Eastman Kodak Company starting in 1991.

The foundation for these first quality documentation seminars was the Information Mapping course, *Developing Procedures, Policies, and Documentation*, first developed by Robert Horn in 1977. Since 1991, Information Mapping, Inc. has worked to improve quality system documentation at a number of other organizations and to expand the quality system content of its seminars for those seeking ISO 9001:2000 certification.

Currently, Information Mapping provides *Mapping ISO 9000 Documentation* seminars throughout the corporate U.S. and in over 20 countries.

Using this Guide

This document is to be used in conjunction with, not as a substitute for, the ISO 9001:2000 International Standard Quality Management System Requirements.

The ISO 9000 series of Standards are published in the U.S. as the American National Standards Institute/American Society for Quality Control Q9000 Series.

Use a registered agency

This document provides interpreted information of the ISO 9000 Standards. If your organization is seeking certification for compliance with the ISO 9001:2000 Standard, contact an accredited registered agency.

Continued on next page

Preface, Continued

Thanks   We wish to acknowledge the help of many people:

- Fen Small, who had the original idea and worked tirelessly to make the first book happen.
- The core, original membership of Team ISO at Information Mapping, including Dan Morgan, Steve Gousie, and Kathy Fast.
- James DiNitto, U.S. Manager for TUV Knowledge Service, for his professional guidance and countless recommendations in his review of this edition.
- Gary Minks, Certification Director for TUV Management Services, for his insight and expert contributions.
- Mitsuharu Matsubara, for his continued interest and input.
- Doug Gorman, President of Information Mapping, Inc, for his continual support and assistance in managing the process.

In addition, we would like to thank many on the staff of Information Mapping, Inc. for their help in ensuring that this document conforms to the principles of the Information Mapping methodology.

And, we are grateful to the many attendees of our ISO 9000 documentation seminars, who have continued to add their ideas to this effort.

Special thanks   We want to give special thanks to Deborah Lakin and Sharon Elkins, who did a great job of making sure the book was up to Information Mapping's high standards.

Finally, we would like to thank Mary R. Trubiano, who worked alongside us every step of the way.

Gerard Paradis
John R. Trubiano

Chapter 1

The ISO 9001:2000 Standard and Certification Process

Overview

Introduction

This chapter describes the ISO 9000 Standards, ISO 9001:2000 concepts, and the ISO Quality Management System certification process.

ISO 9000:2000 Standards

The ISO 9000:2000 Standards together form a set of guidelines for implementing and operating an effective and efficient Quality Management System.

The table below provides a brief description of the ISO 9000:2000 Standards.

ISO 9000:2000 Standards	Purpose
ISO 9000:2000	Describes fundamentals and terminology.
ISO 9001:2000	Specifies the requirements.
ISO 9004:2000	Provides Quality Management System guidelines for performance improvement.

In this chapter

This chapter contains the following topics:

The ISO 9000 Standards

Introduction   This topic provides a description of the requirement, vocabulary, and guideline standards.

Definitions   A *requirement standard* is a standard to which your organization must conform to be certified.

A *guideline standard* is a set of recommendations concerning the establishment of an effective and efficient Quality Management System.

Note: ISO 9000:2000 describes fundamentals of the Quality Management System and specifies the terminology.

Requirement standard, vocabulary, and guidelines   The table below describes the requirement standard, vocabulary, and guidelines of the basic ISO 9000 series.

Type of Standard	Name of Standard	Description
Requirement Standard	ISO 9001:2000	The ISO 9001:2000 Standard contains Quality Management System requirements. This is the only ISO 9000 series Standard against which your Quality Management System can be certified. *Note:* ISO 9002 and ISO 9003 have been eliminated.
Vocabulary	ISO 9000:2000	This standard contains Quality Management System fundamentals and vocabulary.
Guidelines	ISO 9004:2000	This standard contains the Quality Management System guidelines for performance improvement.

Continued on next page

Structure of the ISO 9001:2000 Standard

The table below describes the sections and major topics of the ISO 9001:2000 Standard.

Section	Major Topics
0 Introduction	• 0.1 General • 0.2 Process Approach • 0.3 Relationships with ISO 9004 • 0.4 Compatibility with Other Management Systems
1 Scope	• 1.1 General • 1.2 Application
2 Normative Reference	Related documents
3 Terms and Definitions	Terms and definitions that apply
4 Quality Management System	• 4.1 General Requirements • 4.2 Documentation Requirements
5 Management Responsibility	• 5.1 Management Commitment • 5.2 Customer Focus • 5.3 Quality Policy • 5.4 Planning • 5.5 Responsibility, Authority, and Communication • 5.6 Management Review
6 Resource Management	• 6.1 Provision of Resources • 6.2 Human Resources • 6.3 Infrastructure • 6.4 Work Environment

Continued on next page

The ISO 9000 Standards, Continued

Section	Major Topics
7 Product Realization	• 7.1 Planning of Product Realization • 7.2 Customer-Related Processes • 7.3 Design and/or Development • 7.4 Purchasing • 7.5 Production and Service Provision • 7.6 Control of Measuring and Monitoring Devices
8 Measurement, Analysis, and Improvement	• 8.1 General • 8.2 Monitoring and Measurement • 8.3 Control of Nonconforming Product • 8.4 Analysis of Data • 8.5 Improvement

Overview of the Certification Process

Introduction   This topic provides an overview of how to achieve ISO 9001:2000 certification.

Time to complete   The typical certification process may last from *six to twelve months*.

Factors affecting completion   The amount of time it takes to complete the certification process can depend on several factors, such as

- commitment of management
- complexity and size of the organization
- project management skills of the project team
- documentation skills of the project team
- number and complexity of existing processes, and
- amount and adequacy of existing documentation.

Stages in the process   The table below describes the stages of the typical certification process.

Stage	Name	What Happens?
1	Strategic Planning	Management • displays strong commitment and support for the certification effort • forms a project team • establishes a timeline • assesses training needs regarding ISO 9001:2000 and organizational background, and • selects a registrar.

Continued on next page

Stage	Name	What Happens?
2	Gap Analysis	Corrective action teams evaluate the • existing Quality Management System and documentation against the requirement, and • effective implementation of the Quality Management System.
3	Corrective Action	Corrective action teams institute changes in the Quality Management System as identified in Stage 2.
4	Documentation and Records	Corrective action teams • implement a document structure and control system • institute a control of the records process • revise documents as necessary, and • provide training for changes, additions, and other topics as identified in Stage 1.
5	Implementation	Management • implements and monitors all changes in the Quality Management System • ensures all gaps identified in Stage 2 are closed, and • maintains records of all changes.
6	Pre-Certification Audit	Pre-certification auditor ensures all process controls and documentation are effectively implemented according to the requirement.
7	Registrar Documentation Review	Registrar reviews the Quality Manual, and any other requested documents, as the advance organizer of the certification audit.

Continued on next page

Stages in the process
(continued)

Stage	Name	What Happens?
8	Site Preparation	Management prepares the organization for the registrar and certification audit.
9	Certification Audit	Registrar reviews the Quality Management System and documentation to determine if the Quality Management System meets the ISO 9001:2000 requirements and to determine the effectiveness of the Quality Management System in the meeting of objectives.

Chapter 2

Comparing ISO 9001:2000 and ISO 9001:1994

Overview

Introduction	This chapter compares the requirements of the Quality Management System of ISO 9001:2000 to the previously published ISO 9001:1994 Standard. In addition, this chapter identifies the documentation and records requirements of the 2000 version.

New points of emphasis

Within the framework of the revised ISO 9001:2000 Quality Management System requirements, there are some additions that go beyond and/or add to the 1994 version. These new points include

- increasing focus on the role of top management, particularly around communication
- increasing focus on planning, especially around the development and measurement of Quality Objectives
- establishing and promoting effective continual improvement based on monitoring and analyzing customer satisfaction and Quality Management System data
- reducing the required documented procedures
- increasing focus on the availability of resources
- rearranging the generic requirements of a Quality Management System as linked processes in a process model, and
- establishing a process model that is based on eight Quality Management Principles (referenced in Chapter 3).

Reference: For additional information, refer to page 34.

In this chapter

This chapter contains the following topics.

Topic	See Page
Comparing ISO 9001:2000 and ISO 9001:1994	10
ISO 9001:2000 Documentation and Records Requirements	21

Continued on next page

9

Comparing ISO 9001:2000 and ISO 9001:1994

Introduction   In the ISO 9001:2000 version of the Standard, the 20 elements of ISO 9001:1994 are reorganized into five main sections, including

- Quality Management System
- Management Responsibility
- Resource Management
- Product Realization, and
- Measurement, Analysis, and Improvement.

Comparison table   This table describes the differences between the ISO 9001:2000 and the ISO 9001:1994 Standards.

ISO 9001:2000	ISO 9001:1994	Description of 9001:2000 Differences
1 Scope	1	No significant differences.
1.1 General		Consistently provide product that meets customer and applicable regulatory requirements. Enhance customer satisfaction through the Quality Management System and processes for continual improvement.
1.2 Application		Applies to your organization regardless of type, size, or product. *Important*: Exclusions can be made for items under the requirements of Section 7.
2 Normative Reference	2	No significant differences.

Continued on next page

Comparison table (continued)

ISO 9001:2000	ISO 9001:1994	Description of 9001:2000 Differences
3 Terms and Definitions	3	Use ISO 9000 Quality Management Systems — Fundamentals and Vocabulary. *Note:* Replaces ISO 8402:1994.
4 Quality Management System		
4.1 General Requirements	4.2.1	Ensure availability of resources to monitor processes. Implement and continually improve the effectiveness of the Quality Management System. Identify processes, determine sequence and interactions of processes. Ensure processes are controlled.
4.2 Documentation Requirements		
4.2.1 General	4.2.2	Documentation includes Quality Policy, Quality Objectives, Quality Manual, six Quality Management System procedures, and other documents.
4.2.2 Quality Manual	4.2.1	Include • justification for any exclusions, and • a description of the interactions between the processes.

Continued on next page

Comparison table
(continued)

ISO 9001:2000	ISO 9001:1994	Description of 9001:2000 Differences
4.2.3 Control of Documents	• 4.5.1 • 4.5.2 • 4.5.3	Ensure documents remain legible.
4.2.4 Control of Records	4.16	No significant differences.
5 Management Responsibility		
5.1 Management Commitment	4.1.1	Create an awareness of the importance to meet customer requirements. Demonstrate commitment to the improvement of the Quality Management System.
5.2 Customer Focus	4.3.2	Ensure customer requirements are met with the aim of enhancing customer satisfaction.
5.3 Quality Policy	4.1.1	Include a commitment to continually improve the effectiveness of the Quality Management System. Provide a framework for establishing Quality Objectives.
5.4 Planning		
5.4.1 Quality Objectives	4.1.1	Establish Quality Objectives that are measurable and consistent with the Quality Policy. Quality Objectives include those needed to meet requirements for product/service.

Continued on next page

Comparing ISO 9001:2000 and ISO 9001:1994, Continued

Comparison table
(continued)

ISO 9001:2000	ISO 9001:1994	Description of 9001:2000 Differences
5.4.2 Quality Management System Planning	4.2.3	Identify and plan the activities needed to achieve Quality Objectives. Carry out the plan to meet the requirements given in 4.1. Maintain the integrity of the Quality Management System during changes.
5.5 Responsibility, Authority, and Communication		
5.5.1 Responsibility and Authority	4.1.2.1	Define and communicate responsibility and authority.
5.5.2 Management Representative	4.1.2.3	Ensure the promotion of awareness of customer requirements throughout the organization.
5.5.3 Internal Communication		Communicate between the various levels and functions regarding the Quality Management System's effectiveness.
5.6.1 General	4.1.3	Review to include assessing the opportunities for improvement and the need for changes to the Quality Management System.
5.6.2 Review Input		Include in the review • input customer feedback • process performance • product conformance, and • recommendations for improvement.

Continued on next page

Comparing ISO 9001:2000 and ISO 9001:1994, Continued

Comparison table
(continued)

ISO 9001:2000	ISO 9001:1994	Description of 9001:2000 Differences
5.6.3 Review Output		Include in the review output resource needs for the improvement of product or service related to customer requirements.
6 Resource Management		
6.1 Provision of Resources	4.1.2.2	Ensure the availability of resources to implement and maintain the Quality Management System and to continually improve its effectiveness. This thereby enhances customer satisfaction.
6.2 Human Resources		
6.2.1 General	4.1.2.2	Ensure resources are competent (demonstrated ability to apply knowledge and skills).
6.2.2 Competence, Awareness, and Training	4.18	Evaluate training or other actions taken to determine necessary competence. Ensure personnel are aware of the relevance and importance of their activities, and how they contribute to the achievement of the Quality Objectives.

Continued on next page

14

Comparing ISO 9001:2000 and ISO 9001:1994, Continued

Comparison table
(continued)

ISO 9001:2000	ISO 9001:1994	Description of 9001:2000 Differences
6.3 Infrastructure	4.9	Determine, provide, and maintain • buildings, workspaces, and associated utilities • hardware and software process equipment, and • supporting services, such as transport or communication.
6.4 Work Environment	4.9	Determine and manage the work environment to meet product requirements.
7 Product Realization		
7.1 Planning of Product Realization	• 4.2.3 • 4.10.1	Plan and develop processes needed for product realization. Determine, as appropriate, • Quality Objectives • product requirements • the need to establish processes and documents, and provide resources for product • required verification, validation, monitoring, inspection, and test activities for product and acceptance criteria, and • records needed.

Continued on next page

15

Comparison table
(continued)

ISO 9001:2000	ISO 9001:1994	Description of 9001:2000 Differences
7.2 Customer-Related Processes		
7.2.1 Determination of Requirements Related to the Product	• 4.3.2 • 4.4.4	Determine requirements for delivery and post-delivery activities. Meet regulatory and statutory requirements.
7.2.2 Review of Requirements Related to the Product	• 4.3.2 • 4.3.3 • 4.3.4	No significant differences.
7.2.3 Customer Communication	4.3.2	Determine and implement arrangements for communication regarding product information, inquiries/ contracts, and customer feedback.
7.3 Design and Development		
7.3.1 Design and Development Planning	• 4.4.2 • 4.4.3	No significant differences.
7.3.2 Design and Development Inputs	4.4.4	Generate and retain records of design and development inputs.
7.3.3 Design and Development Outputs	4.4.5	Provide appropriate information for purchasing and production, and for service provision.

Continued on next page

Comparison table (continued)

ISO 9001:2000	ISO 9001:1994	Description of 9001:2000 Differences
7.3.4 Design and Development Review	4.4.6	Evaluate ability to meet requirements. Identify problems and follow-up actions.
7.3.5 Design and Development Verification	4.4.7	Record the necessary actions in the results of the review.
7.3.6 Design and Development Validation	4.4.8	Validate according to planned arrangements. Validate prior to delivery or implementation of product, if possible. Include actions taken in records.
7.3.7 Control of Design and Development Changes	4.4.9	Verify and validate changes. Evaluate the effects changes will have on component parts and delivered product. Include actions taken in records.
7.4 Purchasing		
7.4.1 Purchasing Process	4.6.2	Develop criteria for selection, evaluation, and re-evaluation of suppliers. Record the necessary actions in the results of supplier evaluation.
7.4.2 Purchasing Information	4.6.3	No significant differences.

Continued on next page

Comparison table
(continued)

ISO 9001:2000	ISO 9001:1994	Description of 9001:2000 Differences
7.4.3 Verification of Purchased Product	• 4.6.4 • 4.10.2	No significant differences.
7.5 Production and Service Provision		
7.5.1 Control of Production and Service Provision	• 4.9 • 4.15.6 • 4.19	No significant differences.
7.5.2 Validation of Processes for Production and Service Provision	4.9	Define criteria for review and approval of processes. Re-validate.
7.5.3 Identification and Traceability	• 4.8 • 4.10.5 • 4.12	No significant differences.
7.5.4 Customer Property	4.7	Include confidential information.
7.5.5 Preservation of Product	• 4.15.2 • 4.15.3 • 4.15.4 • 4.15.5	No significant differences.
7.6 Control of Monitoring and Measuring Devices	• 4.11.1 • 4.11.2	No significant differences.

Continued on next page

Comparison table
(continued)

ISO 9001:2000	ISO 9001:1994	Description of 9001:2000 Differences
8 Measurement, Analysis, and Improvement		
8.1 General	• 4.10.1 • 4.17 • 4.20.1 • 4.20.2	Continually improve the effectiveness of the Quality Management System.
8.2 Monitoring and Measurement		
8.2.1 Customer Satisfaction		Monitor information relating to customer perception as to whether the organization has met customer requirements and act on information to achieve objectives.
8.2.2 Internal Audit	4.17	No significant differences.
8.2.3 Monitoring and Measurement of Processes	• 4.17 • 4.20.1 • 4.20.2	Methods need to demonstrate the ability of the process to achieve planned results.
8.2.4 Monitoring and Measurement of Product	• 4.10.2 • 4.10.3 • 4.10.4 • 4.10.5 • 4.20.1 • 4.20.2	No significant differences.
8.3 Control of Non-conforming Product	• 4.13.1 • 4.13.2	No significant differences.

Continued on next page

Comparing ISO 9001:2000 and ISO 9001:1994, Continued

Comparison table
(continued)

ISO 9001:2000	ISO 9001:1994	Description of 9001:2000 Differences
8.4 Analysis of Data	• 4.20.1 • 4.20.2	Demonstrate effectiveness and evaluate where continual improvement of the Quality Management System can be made. Provide information relating to customer satisfaction. Analyze data to provide information.
8.5 Improvement		
8.5.1 Continual Improvement	4.1.3	Continually improve the effectiveness of the Quality Management System.
8.5.2 Corrective Action	• 4.14.1 • 4.14.2	No significant differences.
8.5.3 Preventive Action	• 4.14.1 • 4.14.3	No significant differences.

ISO 9001:2000 Documentation and Records Requirements

Introduction   The ISO 9001:2000 Standard has revised the documentation and records requirements from the 1994 version. In the ISO 9001:2000 version, there are four basic areas that must be addressed, including

- procedures
- records
- processes, and
- documents.

Procedures   This table lists the six ISO 9001:2000 required procedures.

Section	Required Procedure
4.2.3	Control of Documents
4.2.4	Control of Records
8.2.2	Internal Audit
8.3	Control of Nonconforming Product
8.5.2	Corrective Action
8.5.3	Preventive Action

Records   This table describes the ISO 9001:2000 required records.

Section	Required Record	Origin of Record
5.6.1	General	Management reviews.
6.2.2	Competence, awareness, and training	Education, training, skills, and experience.
7.1	Planning of product realization	Processes and resulting product fulfillment requirements.
7.2.2	Review of product requirements	Results of product reviews and actions taken from the reviews.

Continued on next page

ISO 9001:2000 Documentation and Records Requirements, Continued

Records
(continued)

Section	Required Record	Origin of Record
7.3.2	Design and development inputs	Inputs to product requirements.
7.3.4	Design and development review	Results of reviews and actions taken.
7.3.5	Design and development verification	Results of verification and actions taken.
7.3.6	Design and development validation	Results of validation and actions taken.
7.3.7	Control of design and development changes	Results of reviews of changes and actions taken.
7.4.1	Purchasing process	Results of supplier evaluations and actions taken.
7.5.2	Validation of processes for production and service provision	Results of process evaluations and actions taken.
7.5.3	Identification and traceability	Product identification and tracking reports.
7.5.4	Customer property	Lost, damaged, or other unsuitable customer reports and actions taken.
7.6	Control of monitoring and measuring devices	• Reports used for calibration or verification where no standards exist that are traceable to international or national standards, • Validity of previous measuring results when equipment is found not to conform, and • Results of calibration and verification.

Continued on next page

**Records
(continued)**

Section	Required Record	Origin of Record
8.2.2	Internal audit	Results of internal audits, reporting verification follow-up activities and their results.
8.2.4	Monitoring and measurement of product	Product release authorizations.
8.3	Control of nonconforming product	Nonconformity reports, including concessions obtained and actions taken.
8.5.2	Corrective action	Results of actions taken.
8.5.3	Preventive action	Results of actions taken.

Processes

This table describes ISO 9001:2000 processes that typically need to be defined, as applicable.

All key processes in your organization should be defined in some manner.

Section	Processes	Description of Documents
7.1	Planning of product realization	Plans and development processes needed for product realization.
7.2	Customer-related processes	Ensures that customer's needs and requirements are understood and can be met.
7.4.1	Purchasing process	Ensures that purchased product conforms to specified purchase requirements.

Continued on next page

ISO 9001:2000 Documentation and Records Requirements, Continued

Processes (continued)

Section	Processes	Description of Documents
7.5.2	Validation for production and service provisions	Ensures validated and enhanced controls are applied when product/service cannot be verified.
7.6	Control of monitoring and measurement devices	Establishes a process that ensures monitoring and measurement requirements are met.
8.1	General	Plans and implements the monitoring, measurement, analysis, and improvement processes.
8.2.3	Monitoring and measurement of processes	Applies suitable methods for monitoring and measuring the Quality Management System processes.

Note: These methods demonstrate the ability of the processes to achieve planned results. |
| 8.2.4 | Monitoring and measurement of product | Applies suitable methods for monitoring and measuring the product to verify that requirements are met. |
| 8.4 | Analysis of data | Determines, collects, and analyzes appropriate data to provide information on the effectiveness and improvement of the Quality Management System. |

Continued on next page

ISO 9001:2000 Documentation and Records Requirements, Continued

Documents   This table describes the ISO 9001:2000 documents that typically **may** be needed.

Section	Document	What the Document Contains
5.5.1	Responsibility and Authority	Responsibilities and authorities.
5.6	Management review	When, who, what, how, results, and actions needed.
7.3.1	Design/Development Planning	Design and development product outputs as design and development progresses.
7.3.3	Design/Development Outputs	Design and development outputs for purchasing, production, and service provisions.
7.3.7	Control of Design/ Development Changes	Changes in product design and development.
7.4.2	Purchasing Information	Product requirements for • approval, and • ensuring the adequacy of specified purchase requirements.
7.4.3	Verification of Purchased Product	Product verification arrangements and release.
7.5.2	Validation of Processes for Production and Service Provision	Review and approval criteria for product processes.

Continued on next page

ISO 9001:2000 Documentation and Records Requirements, Continued

Required documents

This table describes **required** ISO 9001:2000 documents.

Section	Document	What the Document Contains
4.2.2	Quality Manual	Establishment and maintenance of the description of the interaction between the processes of the Quality Management System.
5.3	Quality Policy	Commitment to • comply with requirements, and • continually improve the effectiveness of the Quality Management System.
5.4.1	Quality Objectives	Establishment of Quality Objectives to be consistent with the Quality Policy and how the Quality Objectives will be measured at relevant functions and levels within the organization.

Chapter 3

What Is a Quality Management System?

Overview

Introduction

This chapter defines and describes what a Quality Management System is, including

- terms
- relationships
- a process model
- Quality Management Principles, and
- quality audits.

In this chapter

This chapter contains the following topics.

Topic	See Page
What Is a Quality Management System?	28
Understanding Quality Audits	33
Quality Management Principles	34

What Is a Quality Management System?

Definition
A *Quality Management System* is that part of the organization's management system that focuses on the achievement of outputs (results) in relation to the Quality Objectives to satisfy the needs, expectations, and requirements of interested parties, as appropriate.

What gets certified?
Your Quality Management System must conform to the ISO 9001:2000 Standard.

Quality Management System terms
This table describes the key terms found in the ISO 9001:2000 Standard relating to a Quality Management System.

Term	Description
Product	The material or service provided. There are four agreed-upon generic product categories: • services • software • hardware, and • processed materials.
Supplier	Your sub-contractor.
Customer	The organization or individual that receives your product/service.
Continual improvement	Used when quality improvement is progressive and the organization actively seeks and pursues improvement opportunities.
Customer satisfaction	Customer-expressed opinions of the degree to which they feel their needs and expectations have been met.

Continued on next page

What Is a Quality Management System?, Continued

Quality Management System terms (continued)

Term	Description
Permissible exclusions	Requirements that neither affect the organization's ability nor absolve it from its responsibility to provide product that meets customer and applicable regulatory requirements. *Note*: Permissible exclusions of any clause may only be made in Section 7.
Audit evidence	Records, verified statements of facts, or other information relevant to an audit.
Competence	Demonstrated ability to apply knowledge and skills.
Review	Determines the suitability, adequacy, and effectiveness of the subject matter to achieve established objectives.

Quality Management System relationships

The diagram below represents the relationship among

- the supplier
- your organization
- your customer, and
- the product.

Continued on next page

What Is a Quality Management System?, Continued

**Meanings of
ISO verbs**

There are two main verbs used throughout the ISO 9001:2000 Standard that relate to your Quality Management System. These verbs are described in the table below.

The verb ...	Means that compliance is ...	And is found primarily in the ...
shall	required	requirement standard.
should	recommended	guideline standards.

Definition

A process is a set of inter-related activities which transforms inputs into outputs. (See ISO 9000:2000, Section 3.4.1.)

Descriptions

Processes are typically

• inputs that provide outputs to other processes, and
• planned and carried out under controlled conditions to add value.

The systematic identification and management of the interaction between such processes are referred to collectively as the process approach.

Continued on next page

What Is a Quality Management System?, Continued

Process approach model

The Quality Management System model below illustrates the integration of processes in a Quality Management System that is continually improving.

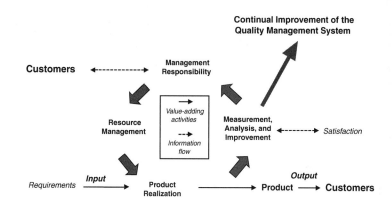

Description of the process model

This table describes the titles of the four major sections of the ISO 9001:2000 Standard and how the Quality Management System process works:

ISO 9001:2000 Section	Title	Description
5	Management Responsibility	Management defines the requirements for new processes to meet customer needs.
6	Resource Management	Management determines the necessary resources and ensures they are employed.
7	Product Realization	The introduction and implementation of product realization processes.
8	Measurement, Analysis, and Improvement	The process results are measured, analyzed, and improved.

Continued on next page

What Is a Quality Management System?, Continued

Outcomes of the process model

The loop is completed by incorporating information into the management review and by authorizing and introducing process changes and improvements.

The customer role is clear when looking at this model. Input for the organization processes is based on customer requirements and expectations.

The results are assessed according to customer feedback. Data collected serves to provide information to improve processes due to more knowledge of customer expectations.

Understanding Quality Audits

Introduction

Your organization may undergo several types of audits:

- first-party audits
- second-party audits, and
- third-party audits.

Third-party
An auditor from an independent agency audits you.

Second-party
Your customer audits you or your organization audits your supplier.

First-party
You audit yourself.

Definition

An *audit* is an objective evaluation of your Quality Management System and documentation.

First-Party audit

A *first-party audit* is an internal audit performed by your organization on its own Quality Management System.

Second-Party audit

A *second-party audit* is a Quality Management System audit performed by your customer on your organization or your organization on your supplier.

Third-Party audit

A *third-party audit* is a Quality Management System audit performed by an independent agency, such as a registrar, on your organization to achieve certification for the ISO 9001:2000 Standard.

The third-party auditor must ensure objectivity and impartiality to both your customer and your organization. The customer or your organization cannot perform third-party audits.

Continued on next page

Quality Management Principles

Introduction   ISO 9001:2000 is based on Quality Management System Principles.

These Quality Management Principles are meant to help an organization achieve the goals of their Quality Objectives.

There are eight Quality Management Principles in ISO 9001:2000

- Customer-Focused Organizations
- Leadership
- Involvement of People
- Process Approach
- System Approach to Management
- Continual Improvement
- Factual Approach to Decision-Making, and Mutually Beneficial Supplier Relationships.

Results of using the eight principles   This table describes the organizational actions that result from using the eight Quality Management Principles and refers to an example from the ISO 9001:2000 Standard.

When the Organization Applies the Principle of ...	Then the Organization is ...	ISO 9001:2000 Example
Customer-Focus	• communicating customer needs throughout the organization • measuring customer satisfaction and acting on results, and • managing customer relationships.	5.2

Continued on next page

Quality Management Principles, Continued

Results of using
the eight principles
(continued)

When the Organization Applies the Principle of ...	Then the Organization is ...	ISO 9001:2000 Example
Leadership	• being proactive and leading by example, and • providing people with resources and the freedom to act responsibly and with accountability.	5
Involvement of People	• actively seeking opportunities to make improvements, and • being innovative and creative in furthering the organization's objectives.	6.2.2
Process Approach	• defining the process to achieve the desired result • identifying and measuring the inputs and outputs of the process, and • identifying the interfaces of the process with the functions of the organization.	0.2
System Approach to Management	• defining the system by identifying or developing the processes that affect a given objective, and • structuring the system to achieve the objective in the most efficient way.	4.1
Continual Improvement	• making continual improvement of products, processes, and systems an objective for every individual in the organization, and • promoting prevention-based activities.	• 5.3B • 8.5.1

Continued on next page

Quality Management Principles, Continued

When the Organization Applies the Principle of ...	Then the Organization is ...	ISO 9001:2000 Example
Factual Approach to Decision-Making	• analyzing the data and information using valid methods, and • making decisions and taking actions based on the results.	8.4
Mutually Beneficial Supplier Relationships	• creating clear and open communications, and • jointly establishing a clear understanding of customer needs.	7.4

Chapter 4

Quality Management System

Overview

Introduction   This chapter discusses the general requirements and documentation requirements of the Quality Management System.

In this chapter   This chapter covers the following Quality Management System requirements in general terms:

Topic	ISO Section	See Page
General Requirements	4.1	38
Documentation Requirements	4.2	39
• General	4.2.1	39
• Quality Manual	4.2.2	41
• Control of Documents	4.2.3	43
• Control of Records	4.2.4	45

4.1 General Requirements

Requirements   Your organization must establish, document, implement, maintain, and continually improve a Quality Management System in accordance with the ISO 9001:2000 Standard.

What this means   Having a Quality Management System as part of the overall management system is very important. By using the ISO 9001:2000 Standard, management can improve the performance of the organization.

Implementation process   The table below describes a typical process for implementing an organization's Quality Management System.

Stage	Description
1	Identifies the processes needed.
2	Determines the sequences and interactions of those processes.
3	Determines criteria and methods for those processes.
4	Ensures availability of resources and information.
5	Measures, monitors, and analyzes activities used to ensure conformity to specified requirements and attain continual improvement.
6	Implements actions to achieve planned results and continual improvement.

4.2 Documentation Requirements

4.2.1 General

Requirements

Your Quality Management System documentation must include

- a Quality Manual
- documented statements of Quality Policy and Quality Objectives
- documented procedures required in the ISO 9001:2000 Standard
- other documents required by your organization to ensure the effective planning, operation, and control of its processes, and
- records.

What this means

Organizational policy, objectives, process, and procedure documentation can be a functional tool for controlling the Quality Management System.

ISO documents **can** be organized into four basic categories *or levels* based on the purpose of the document for the user, as described in the table below.

Level	Purpose
1	The Quality Manual specifies the Quality Management System of an organization, addresses management policies, and describes the interactions between the processes. *Note*: The Quality Manual can vary in detail to suit the organization.
2	Describes how the organization's quality management policies are implemented, along with the cross-functional processes that make them happen.
3	Provides task-based instructions to ensure the Level 2 processes work.
4	The records provide evidence that the system is operated as it is documented and is effective.

Continued on next page

4.2 Documentation Requirements, Continued

4.2.1 General, Continued

What this means
(continued)

Reference: For a more detailed description of the four levels, see page 156.

Evidence

The list of evidence required for this section of the Standard includes

- procedures required by ISO 9001:2000 Standard
- Quality Manual
- Quality Policy
- Quality Objectives, and
- other documents required by your organization.

Auditor questions

Typical questions an auditor might ask for this section of the Standard include:

- Where are your procedures required by the Standard?
- What is your documented Quality Policy?
- What are your documented Quality Objectives?
- What is included in your documented Quality Management System?

Continued on next page

4.2 Documentation Requirements, Continued

4.2.2 Quality Manual

Requirements   A Quality Manual must be established and maintained to include the following:

- the scope of the Quality Management System
- documented procedures or references to the system, and
- a description of the sequence and interaction between the processes.

What this means   Establish a Quality Manual that describes the interaction between the processes of your Quality Management System. This would include showing all inputs and outputs of major processes.

Inclusions/ Exclusions   The Quality Manual needs to include

- the scope of the Quality Management System
- justification for exclusions, if any for the organization, and
- a description of the interactions between key processes.

Note: The output of one process may be the input for another process.

Required documentation

A documented Quality Manual that includes documented procedures or references to them.

Rationale: This documentation serves as a basis for implementation and maintenance of the system.

Control of the Quality Manual   The Quality Manual needs to be controlled as defined in the organization's document control procedure.

Continued on next page

4.2 Documentation Requirements, Continued

4.2.2 Quality Manual, Continued

Evidence

The list of evidence required for this section of the Standard is a Quality Manual that includes

- a description of Quality Management System
- documented Quality Management System procedures or references to them
- a description of the interaction, such as Process Map, between the processes of the Quality Management System, and
- the Quality Management System scope and justification detailed for any exclusions.

Auditor questions

Typical questions an auditor might ask for this section of the Standard include:

- How is your Quality Manual controlled?
- Who approves changes to your Quality Manual?
- Does your Quality Manual include the scope of your Quality Management System?
- Are your documented processes, procedures, and interactions included or referenced?

Continued on next page

4.2.3 Control of Documents

Requirements

Documents required for the Quality Management System must be controlled. This includes documents defined as records. A documented procedure must be established to address this control.

Definition

Documents contain approved information to ensure that your Quality Management System's policies, processes, and procedures are carried out in the proper manner.

Note: Records documents state the results achieved, or provide evidence of activities performed.

What this means

Control of documents includes

- approving for adequacy prior to issue
- reviewing and updating as needed
- identifying current revisions
- ensuring documents are available where needed, and
- ensuring legibility and identification.

Required documentation

Document a procedure that addresses approval, review, updates, current revisions, availability, legibility, and identification.

Approval

Authorized personnel need to approve new and revised documents for the information prior to release to the organization.

Continued on next page

4.2.3 Control of Documents, Continued

Document review New and revised documents need to be reviewed, updated, and re-approved by authorized personnel, as necessary, for the improvement of the Quality Management System.

Revision control New and revised documents need to be identified with a current revision status and changes indicated in some form of change notice. This ensures documents are being used where they are needed, always legible, and readily identified.

External documents Ensure external documents that are needed for the Quality Management System are identified and distributed under control.

Examples include

- standards
- software for equipment operation, and
- customer specifications.

Obsolete documents Ensure obsolete documents are not used unintentionally and are promptly removed from all points of use. If they are retained for any purpose, they should be suitably identified.

Records Documents defined as records must be controlled.

Reference: See 4.2.4, Control of Records

Continued on next page

4.2.3 Control of Documents, Continued

Evidence

The list of evidence required for this section of the Standard includes a documented procedure that addresses approval, review, revision, availability, legibility, and identification of the organization's controlled documents. External documents and obsolete documents need to be addressed in this procedure.

Additional evidence includes

- document control of all Quality Management System documents, and
- effective process and implementation of document control.

Auditor questions

Typical questions that may be asked by an auditor include:

- What is your document control process?
- Where is your document control procedure?
- Who approves documents for adequacy prior to issue?
- How are changes identified?
- How are obsolete documents controlled?

Continued on next page

4.2 Documentation Requirements, Continued

4.2.4 Control of Records

Requirements

Records must be maintained to provide evidence of conformance to requirements and effective operation of the Quality Management System.

A documented procedure must be established for the identification, storage, retrieval, protection, retention time, and disposition of records.

Records must be legible.

What this means

Retain records of the Quality Management System's performance. The records need to be controlled, maintained, and protected so that your organization has control of the records. A documented record control procedure must address how the records will be controlled.

Required documentation

Document procedures that address record

* identification
* storage
* retrieval
* protection
* retention time, and
* disposition.

Continued on next page

4.2 Documentation Requirements, Continued

4.2.4 Control of Records, Continued

Definition

Records contain information on what has happened in the Quality Management System in the past.

Records need to be maintained and controlled to

- provide evidence that the Quality Management System has been implemented
- show conformance to requirements
- provide knowledge for performance, and
- show improvement of the Quality Management System.

Many elements refer to necessary or subsequent actions; for these records, include follow-up actions.

Example: Records of actions taken to resolve a discrepancy between a quote and a customer order.

Retrieving records

Records need to be retrievable during the time of their review and use for those who need them.

Protecting records

Records need to be protected from deterioration, damage, and loss.

Retention time

Records need to have a retention time established so that, at the end of the retention time, the records can be destroyed.

Continued on next page

4.2 Documentation Requirements, Continued

4.2.4 Control of Records, Continued

Process for controlling records

The table below describes processes for controlling records.

Stage	What Happens
1 Identification	Identifies individual records and retention needs.
2 Protection	Shields from loss, damages, etc.
3 Storage	Places records in locations and provides for a filing method during the required archival part of an individual record's life.
4 Retrieval	Recovers from storage.
5 Retention	Retains until disposition.
6 Disposition	Disposes of individual record when it is no longer needed.

Evidence

The list of evidence required for this section of the Standard includes the procedure that addresses control, maintenance, identification, storage, retrieval, protection, retention time, and disposition of records.

Auditor questions

Typical questions that may be asked by an auditor include:

- Where is your record control procedure?
- How are your records protected from deterioration?
- How are your records stored?
- How are your records identified?
- Where is the defined retention time for your records?

Chapter 5

Management Responsibility

Introduction   This chapter discusses top management's role in the development of the Quality Management System.

In this chapter   This chapter contains the following topics:

Topic	Section	See Page
Management Commitment	5.1	50
Customer Focus	5.2	52
Quality Policy	5.3	53
Planning	5.4	55
• Quality Objectives	5.4.1	55
• Quality Management System Planning	5.4.2	57
Responsibility, Authority, and Communication	5.5	59
• Responsibility and Authority	5.5.1	59
• Management Representative	5.5.2	61
• Internal Communication	5.5.3	63
Management Review	5.6	65
• General	5.6.1	65
• Review Input	5.6.2	67
• Review Output	5.6.3	70

5.1 Management Commitment

Requirements	Top management must provide evidence of its commitment to the development and continual improvement of the Quality Management System.
What this means	Take an active and leading role in the development, implementation, and maintenance of the five requirements, including • communication • establishing the Quality Policy • establishing the Quality Objectives • conducting management reviews, and • allocating resources.
Communicate management commitment	Set and communicate directions related to achieving and continually improving customer satisfaction through requirements of the customers' inputs.
Set Quality Policy/Objectives	Set the Quality Policy and Quality Objectives and lead the organization to • increased awareness, motivation, and involvement • an approach for measurement of the organization's performance, and • continual improvement to verify that Quality Objectives are achieved.
Management review	Review and monitor performance information, such as process performance and customer satisfaction. Use process performance and customer satisfaction as inputs to management review to ensure that continual improvement is the driver for organizational development.

Continued on next page

5.1 Management Commitment, Continued

Resources

Consider the resources and communication needed to ensure that the Quality Management System is maintained and developed as the organization's structure changes.

Evidence

The list of evidence required for this section of the Standard should demonstrate that top management is

- communicating about customer requirements and regulatory and statutory requirements
- establishing a Quality Policy and Quality Objectives
- conducting management reviews
- providing necessary resources to the Quality Management System, and
- committing to continually improve the Quality Management System.

Auditor questions

Typical questions that may be asked by an auditor include:

- How are customer requirements and regulatory and statutory requirements communicated and met?
- What is your Quality Policy?
- What are your Quality Objectives?
- How do you communicate Quality Objectives to your employees?
- What records do you keep from management reviews?
- How does top management ensure the availability of resources?
- How does top management establish continual improvement as an objective for the processes of the organization?

5.2 Customer Focus

Requirements Top management must ensure that customer needs and expectations are determined, converted into requirements, and met with the expectation of enhancing customer satisfaction.

What this means Identify customer needs and expectations, and translate the needs into requirements with the aim of meeting customer satisfaction.

Identifying needs Understand current and future needs and expectations of customers by gathering data.

Translating needs into requirements Identify a process to translate customer needs and expectations into requirements to pursue customer satisfaction.

Evidence The list of evidence required for this section of the Standard should demonstrate top management's commitment to ensure that customer needs and expectations are

- determined
- turned into requirements, and
- met.

Auditor questions Typical questions that may be asked by an auditor include:

- How do you determine your customers' needs?
- How do you turn your customers' needs into requirements?
- How are the requirements fulfilled?
- What regulatory and statutory requirements do you need to consider?

5.3 Quality Policy

Requirements	Top management must ensure that the Quality Policy

  - is appropriate (consistent) to the purpose of the organization
  - includes a commitment to meeting requirements and continual improvement
  - provides a framework for establishing and reviewing Quality Objectives
  - is communicated and understood at appropriate levels in the organization, and
  - is reviewed for continuing suitability.

What this means	Ensure that the Quality Policy

  - is periodically reviewed and revised as necessary to be consistent with the organization's business policies
  - addresses the needs of all parties, and
  - considers opportunities for continual improvement.

Appropriate	The Quality Policy needs to be aligned with the organization's overall business policies. This is done by demonstrating top management's commitment to quality and continual improvement. It should include customer satisfaction as one of its goals.

Establishing Quality Objectives	Quality Objectives are established from the Quality Policy and reviewed and revised as necessary.

Communicating the Quality Policy	Ensure that the Quality Policy is communicated and understood within the organization.

Continued on next page

5.3 Quality Policy, Continued

Evidence

The list of evidence required for this section of the Standard includes

- appropriateness of the Quality Policy to the purpose of the organization
- commitment to meeting Quality Policy requirements and continual improvement
- reviewing the Quality Policy for suitability
- communicating the Quality Policy
- ensuring the Quality Policy is understood, and
- controlling the Quality Policy.

Auditor questions

Typical questions that may be asked by an auditor include:

- What is your Quality Policy?
- How does the Quality Policy relate to you and your job?
- How does your management show commitment to quality?
- How do you ensure that your Quality Policy is understood and implemented within the organization?
- How does your Quality Policy comply with continually improving the effectiveness of the Quality Management System?
- How do you ensure that the Quality Policy is being met?

5.4 Planning

5.4.1 Quality Objectives

Requirements	Top management must ensure that Quality Objectives • are established • are measurable and consistent with the Quality Policy, including the commitment to continual improvement, and • meet the requirements for the product.
What this means	Establish measurable Quality Objectives during the planning process. They must demonstrate a commitment to continual improvement, while meeting your customers' product requirements.
Establish and communicate Objectives	Ensure the Quality Objectives • permeate throughout the organization, and • are clearly communicated to the relevant functions and levels within the organization. Employees need to be able to understand and implement the Quality Objectives in their individual roles.
Measurable	Quality Objectives should be measurable in order for current product, process performance, and satisfaction of all interested parties to be considered.
Evidence	The list of evidence required for this section of the Standard should demonstrate that the Quality Objectives • are established and measurable at relevant functions/levels • commit to continual improvement, and • address product requirements.

Continued on next page

5.4 Planning, Continued

5.4.1 Quality Objectives, Continued

Auditor questions Typical questions that may be asked by an auditor include:

- How are your Quality Objectives measured?
- How are your Quality Objectives established at relevant functions and levels within the organization?
- How are your Quality Objectives measurable and consistent with the Quality Policy?

Continued on next page

5.4 Planning, Continued

5.4.2 Quality Management System Planning

Requirements

Top management must ensure that the

- planning of the processes of the Quality Management System is carried out to meet requirements, including the Quality Objectives, and
- output of quality planning defines the necessary processes.

Planning must ensure that change is conducted in a controlled manner and that the integrity of the Quality Management System is maintained during a change.

What this means

Ensure that the essential activities and resources are in place to satisfy the Quality Policy, Quality Objectives, and requirements of the Quality Management System.

Measurement processes

Establish processes that measure the performance of the Quality Management System in the quality planning.

Define processes

Top management needs to define the quality planning processes needed.

Recommended documentation

Quality planning should be documented, reviewed, and revised as necessary.

Quality planning results

Ensure that the outputs of quality planning identify the

- resources
- skills
- knowledge
- responsibility, and
- authority for executing improvement plans.

Continued on next page

5.4.2 Quality Management System Planning, Continued

Continual improvement

Ensure that the outputs of quality planning identify improvement approaches, methodology, tools, and indicators for performance achievement, as appropriate.

Evidence

The list of evidence required for this section of the Standard should demonstrate that top management ensures that

- the resources needed to achieve Quality Objectives are identified and planned
- output of quality planning is available, and
- quality planning includes processes and continual improvement.

Auditor questions

Typical questions that may be asked by an auditor include:

- Is the output of your quality planning documented?
- How does your quality planning address resources, processes, continual improvement, and change control?

5.5 Responsibility, Authority, and Communication

5.5.1 Responsibility and Authority

Requirements	Top management must administer a Quality Management System that designates • responsibility • authority, and • communication of responsibilities and authority. Each of these requirements is discussed individually in this topic.
Requirements	Top management must define the functions within the organization, including responsibilities and authorities. Top management must communicate these responsibilities to the organization.
What this means	Ensure that all people are given the authority and responsibilities to enable them to assist in the achievement of the Quality Objectives. This helps to establish involvement and commitment of the people throughout the organization to implement and maintain the Quality Management System effectively and efficiently.
Responsibilities	Communicate and define the responsibilities and that all the functions have the authority to perform those responsibilities within the Quality Management System.
Evidence	The evidence required for this section of the Standard includes defined functions within the organization that are given authority and responsibility to achieve the Quality Objectives.

Continued on next page

5.5 Responsibility, Authority, and Communication, Continued

5.5.1 Responsibility and Authority, Continued

Auditor questions   Typical questions that may be asked by an auditor include:

- How are functional responsibilities defined and communicated?
- How are people given authority and responsibility to achieve the Quality Objectives?

Continued on next page

5.5 Responsibility, Authority, and Communication, Continued

5.5.2 Management Representative

Requirements	Top management must appoint a member of management who has responsibility and authority for • ensuring that quality processes are established and maintained • reporting to top management on the performance of the Quality Management System, including needs for improvement, and • promoting awareness of customer requirements throughout the organization.
What this means	Appoint a management representative and give the representative the authority to manage, monitor, evaluate, and coordinate the Quality Management System processes. This person reports to top management and communicates with customers and other interested parties on matters pertaining to the Quality Management System.
Responsibility of the management representative	The management representative must • ensure that all processes in the Quality Management System are established and maintained to enhance effective and efficient operations • report Quality Management System performance to top management, and • communicate customer requirements to all levels of the organization.

Continued on next page

Evidence

The list of evidence required for this section of the Standard should demonstrate that the management representative

- is appointed by top management
- ensures that the processes of the Quality Management System are established and maintained
- reports the performance and needs for improvement of the Quality Management System to top management, and
- promotes awareness of customer requirements.

Auditor questions

Typical questions that may be asked by an auditor include:

- Who is your management representative?
- How does your management representative ensure that the processes of the Quality Management System are established and maintained?
- How does your management representative promote awareness of customer requirements?

Continued on next page

5.5 Responsibility, Authority, and Communication, Continued

5.5.3 Internal Communication

Requirements	Your organization must ensure communication between its various levels and functions regarding the effectiveness of the Quality Management System.

What this means	The organization needs to define, develop, and implement processes for the communication of quality requirements, objectives, and accomplishments.

These communications are to be distributed to all levels of the organization. |

What communi-cation to include	Communication to all levels of the organization can include

• team briefings
• memos
• reports
• meeting minutes
• notice-boards
• in-house journals/magazines
• audio-visual, and
• electronic media.

When information about quality requirements, Quality Objectives, and quality accomplishments are known through-out the organization, this involves all people in the improve-ment of the Quality Management System. |

Evidence	The list of evidence required for this section of the Standard includes

• communications between all levels and functions of the organization, and
• the effectiveness of those communications. |

Continued on next page

5.5 Responsibility, Authority, and Communication, Continued

5.5.3 Internal Communication, Continued

Auditor questions Typical questions that may be asked by an auditor include:

- How are the quality requirements communicated?
- How are the Quality Objectives communicated?
- How are people involved in the achievement of the Quality Objectives?

5.6. Management Review

5.6.1 General

Requirements	Top management must review the Quality Management System at planned intervals to ensure its continuing suitability, adequacy, and effectiveness.
	The review must evaluate the need for changes to the organization's Quality Management System, including the Quality Policy and Quality Objectives.
	Records from management reviews need to be maintained.
Definition	*Management review* is the process of periodically analyzing the Quality Management System for suitability and effectiveness.
What this means	Establish a process to conduct a periodic management review of the Quality Management System to evaluate its effectiveness and efficiency.
Review the system	Review the Quality Management System at periodic intervals to
	• ensure its continuing suitability and adequacy, and • establish how often the Quality Management System is reviewed.
Purpose of the review	The review is used to ensure that the Quality Management System
	• has continuing suitability • is adequate, and • is effective enough to facilitate and promote continuous improvement.

Continued on next page

5.6. Management Review, Continued

5.6.1 General, Continued

Evaluate need for changes

Ensure that the Quality Management System is evaluated to see if there is a need to change the Quality Policy and Quality Objectives as market strategies, environmental, and technological issues change.

Required records

Management's review of records needs to show information on

• specific inputs
• specific outputs, and
• decisions and resulting actions.

Evidence

The list of evidence required for this section of the Standard includes

• conducting periodic management reviews
• reviewing the effectiveness of the Quality Management System, and
• reviewing the Quality Management System to determine the need to change the Quality Policy and/or Objectives.

Auditor questions

Typical questions that may be asked by an auditor include:

• When are management reviews conducted?
• How is the Quality Management System reviewed for effectiveness?
• How do you evaluate the need for changes to the Quality Management System in regard to the Quality Policy and Quality Objectives?

Continued on next page

5.6. Management Review, Continued

5.6.2 Review Input

Requirements

Inputs to a management review must include current performance and improvement opportunities related to

- results of audits
- customer feedback
- process performance and product conformance
- status of preventive and corrective actions
- follow-up actions from earlier management reviews
- changes that could affect the Quality Management System, and
- recommendations for improvement.

What this means

At the management review, your organization needs to review the results of the Quality Management System

- audits
- customer feedback
- process performance and product conformance
- status of preventive and corrective actions
- follow-up actions from earlier management reviews, and
- changes that could affect the Quality Management System.

These items need to be included in the agenda of the management review so that observations, conclusions, and recommendations can be documented for necessary action.

Continued on next page

5.6.2 Review Input, Continued

Sources of review   The table below describes the sources that top management needs to review in the Quality Management System during a management review.

Source of Reviews	Description
Audits	All internal, customer, and third-party audit results.
Customer feedback	Customer feedback. Measurements of satisfaction.
Analysis of process and product	Analysis of process performance and product conformances to improve quality.
Corrective and preventive actions	Status of corrective and preventive actions. The implementation and effectiveness of corrective and preventive actions should be assessed.
Follow-up actions	Assessment of each action item's status from the last review.
System changes	Changes that could affect the Quality Management System. Examples include • outputs of research and development • quality concepts • environmental conditions, and • relevant statutory and regulatory changes.

Evidence   The agenda at a management review meeting is the evidence required for this section of the Standard.

Continued on next page

5.6. Management Review, Continued

5.6.2 Review Input, Continued

Auditor questions   Typical questions that may be asked by an auditor include:

- What information is presented for review at your management review?
- How do you obtain customer feedback?
- How do you determine what measurements are not acceptable?
- How do you decide on recommendations for improvement?

Continued on next page

5.6. Management Review, Continued

5.6.3 Review Output

Requirements	Outputs from the management review must include actions related to

• improvement of the Quality Management System and its processes
• improvement of product, and
• resource needs.

Results of management reviews must be recorded.

What this means	The actions taken as a result of a management review should add value to your organization. They are a management view of

• how you are doing against your Quality Policy and Quality Objectives
• the overall effectiveness of the Quality Management System, and
• what actions need to be taken for improvement.

The organization needs to record the results of each management review.

Actions and results	The actions taken as a result of a management review need to

• create an environment for quality improvement
• relate to improvement of the product, and
• help plan for future resources.

Continued on next page

5.6. Management Review, Continued

5.6.3 Review Output, Continued

Evidence

The list of evidence required for this section of the Standard includes

- improvement of the Quality Management System and its processes
- improvement of product related to customer requirements, and
- resource needs.

Auditor questions   Typical questions that may be asked by an auditor include:

- Where are your management review records?
- Where are the results of the management reviews recorded?
- What methods do you use to determine the effectiveness of your Quality Management System?
- Do the records provide evidence that inputs were addressed?

Reference: See 5.6.2, Review Input.

Chapter 6

Resource Management

Overview

Introduction   This chapter describes how to manage the essential resources to implement the organization's Quality Management System's strategies and objectives.

In this chapter   This chapter contains the following topics.

Topic	Section	See Page
Provision of Resources	6.1	74
Human Resources	6.2	76
• General	6.2.1	76
• Competence, Awareness, and Training	6.2.2	77
Infrastructure	6.3	79
Work Environment	6.4	81

6.1 Provision of Resources

Requirements　Your organization must determine and provide, in a timely manner, the resources needed to

- implement and improve the processes of the Quality Management System, and
- address customer satisfaction.

What this means　Identify and make available the following resources in a timely manner

- people
- suppliers
- information
- infrastructure
- work environment, and
- financial resources.

This requirement supports the Quality Management System processes designed to implement, improve, and address customer satisfaction needs.

Purpose of providing resources　Have the resources available to

- encourage innovative continual improvement, and
- address customer satisfaction.

Training resources　Consider training, education, and learning to help provide competence for current and future resources.

Evidence　The list of evidence required for this section of the Standard includes timely planning and allocation of resources to

- implement and improve processes
- address customer satisfaction
- identify resource requirements, and
- achieve objectives.

Continued on next page

6.1 Provision of Resources, Continued

Auditor questions   Typical questions that may be asked by an auditor include:

- How are resources identified?
- How are resources allocated?
- How are resources planned for and made available in a timely manner?
- How do you determine if you have adequate resources to enhance customer satisfaction by meeting customer requirements?

6.2 Human Resources

6.2.1 General

Requirements

Your organization must ensure that the personnel assigned to various responsibilities defined in the Quality Management System are competent on the basis of applicable education, training, skills, and experience.

What this means

Assign personnel to the Quality Management System based on their competence as related to their education, training, skills, experience, and demonstrated ability to apply knowledge and skills.

Evidence

The list of evidence required for this section of the Standard should demonstrate that personnel assigned to the Quality Management System are competent on the basis of

- education
- training
- skill, and
- experience.

The resources should demonstrate an ability to apply knowledge and skills.

Auditor question

A typical question that may be asked by an auditor is: How do you determine that personnel assigned to the Quality Management System are competent?

Continued on next page

6.2 Human Resources, Continued

6.2.2 Competence, Awareness, and Training

Requirements	Your organization must • identify competency needs • provide training to satisfy competency • evaluate the effectiveness of the training provided • ensure personnel know how they contribute to the achievement of the Quality Objectives, and • maintain appropriate records of education, experience, training, and qualifications.
What this means	To ensure competency, awareness, and training • identify the competency required for each quality activity • provide the training identified for the competency • measure the effectiveness of the training • increase awareness of personnel on how their activities contribute to the achievement of the Quality Objectives, and • keep records of education, experience, training, and skills.
Identify competency	Identify competency for current and future needs of the organization that affect quality.
Provide training	Analyze the training needs of all your personnel and design training plans for them. The training plans should • include training objectives • emphasize meeting customer requirements, and • include awareness of impact to the organization when personnel fail to meet the Quality Objectives.
Evaluate training	Evaluate the training to see if it meets the training objectives.

Continued on next page

6.2 Human Resources, Continued

6.2.2 Competence, Awareness, and Training, Continued

Ensure awareness   Ensure that personnel are knowledgeable about how their quality activities contribute to the achievement of the organization's Quality Objectives.

Required records   Keep records of skills, education, experience, training, and qualifications.

Evidence   The list of evidence needed for this section of the Standard should demonstrate that the organization

- identifies competency needs for personnel involved in the Quality Management System
- provides necessary training or takes actions to satisfy these needs
- evaluates the effectiveness of the training
- ensures personnel awareness and evidence of how their quality activities contribute to the achievement of the Quality Objectives, and
- maintains records to show how personnel are competent to do their tasks.

Auditor questions   Typical questions that may be asked by an auditor include:

- How do you identify competency for personnel who perform quality activities?
- How do you provide training based on competency needs?
- How do you evaluate the effectiveness of the training provided?
- How do you ensure that personnel are aware of the importance of their Quality Objectives and how they contribute to the achievement of the organization's Quality Objectives?
- What training records do you maintain?

5.3 Infrastructure

Requirements	Your organization must identify, provide, and maintain the infrastructure it needs to achieve conformity of product.
What this means	Identify, provide, and maintain the infrastructure as a foundation for the operation. This requirement supports the relationship of the • workspace and associated infrastructure • equipment • hardware and software, and • supporting services.
Use of workspace and equipment	The workspace and associated facilities need to be appropriated for the achievement of the Quality Policy and Quality Objectives.
Equipment	Ensure that equipment, hardware, and software continue to meet the needs of the organization and are maintained based on their criticality and usage.
Associated issues	Consider environmental issues, such as conservation, pollution, waste, and recycling. The organization should consider associated risks and include strategies to maintain the quality of products.
Evidence	The list of evidence required for this section of the Standard should demonstrate that the organization has identified, provided, and maintained the • workspace and associated facilities • equipment, hardware, and software, and • associated issues.

Continued on next page

6.3 Infrastructure, Continued

Auditor questions   Typical questions that may be asked by an auditor include:

- How do you ensure the workspace and associated facilities are adequate to achieve product conformity?
- How do you maintain adequate facilities?

5.4 Work Environment

Requirements	Your organization must identify and manage the human and physical factors of the work environment needed to achieve conformity of products and/or services.
What this means	Provide an environment that influences the motivation, satisfaction, and performance of people, which in turn may enhance the performance of the organization.
Consider human factors	Allow creative work methodologies and opportunities to realize the potential of all people. Consider safety rules and guidance, protective equipment, ergonomics, and special facilities for handicapped personnel in the organization.
Consider physical factors	Consider heat, noise, light, hygiene, humidity, cleanliness, vibration, pollution, and airflow in the work environment.

Evidence

The list of evidence required for this section of the Standard should demonstrate that the organization identifies and manages the work environment for

- creative work methods, safety, rules, and
- hygiene, cleanliness, noise.

Auditor questions

Typical questions that may be asked by an auditor include:

- How are human factors identified and managed in the organization to achieve conformity of product and/or service?
- How are physical factors identified and managed in the organization to achieve conformity of product and/or service?

Chapter 7

Product Realization

Overview

Introduction   This chapter describes the processes and subprocesses
                         required to achieve product realization.

In this chapter   This chapter contains the following topics.

7.1 Planning of Product Realization

Requirements   Your organization must plan the product realization processes so that they are consistent with the other requirements of the organization's Quality Management System and the output of this planning is in a form suitable for the organization's method of operation.

Note: Documentation that describes how the processes of the Quality Management System are applied to a specific product, project, or contract may be referred to as a Quality Plan.

What this means   Plan, identify, and document the processes required to produce products to satisfy the customer's and any other interested party's requirements.

Measuring Quality Objectives   Determine and plan how you will measure your Quality Objectives and product requirements.

Establish processes   Plan how you will establish realization processes and the support processes that consist of inputs, activities, and outputs. The interdependence of product realization and support processes can result in networks of processes.

Definitions   *Realization processes* result in the products of the organization that add value.

Support processes include management processes that are necessary to the organization, but do not directly add value.

Required process   Establish the output of the planning of realization processes and sub-processes. This planning should include documentation, resources, and facilities, as appropriate.

Continued on next page

7.1 Planning of Product Realization, Continued

Managing processes

Plan how to manage the processes by verifying, validating, controlling, and monitoring the activities within each process. This includes defining acceptable criteria for evaluating the processes.

Maintaining records

Plan which records will be maintained to provide confidence that the processes and product conform to the requirements.

Evidence

The list of evidence required for this section of the Standard should show planning that addresses

- Quality Objectives and product requirements
- the need to
  - establish processes
  - document processes, and
  - provide resources
- facilities specific to the product
- verification and validation activities, and the acceptable criteria
- records necessary to provide evidence of conformity of processes, and
- customer service that fulfills requirements.

Auditor questions   Typical questions that may be asked by an auditor include:

- How do you determine the processes to produce product?
- How do you determine the validation of processes?
- How do you determine the verification of product?
- How do you determine the acceptance criteria for product?
- How do you determine what records are needed?

7.2 Customer-Related Processes

7.2.1 Determination of Product Requirements

Requirements	Your organization must determine customer requirements and establish a process to understand the customer requirements that are specified and not specified, but necessary for use. These processes should include identification and review of relevant information.

What this means	Plan and establish a process to understand the needs and expectations of all parties. This includes product requirements defined by the customer and other interested parties, and those not defined that are needed for known or intended use.

Determine

- availability
- delivery
- product support
- regulatory, and
- statutory requirements. |

Consider the customer's role	Determine customer product realization requirements, including

- availability
- delivery, and
- support. |

Regulatory obligations	Determine and respond to regulatory and statutory obligations where applicable.

Continued on next page

7.2.1 Determination of Product Requirements, Continued

Evidence

The list of evidence required for this section of the Standard includes

- product requirements specified by the customer
- product requirements not specified by the customer, but needed for intended use
- availability, delivery, and support of those products, and
- regulatory and statutory obligations.

Auditor questions

Typical questions that may be asked by an auditor include:

- How have you planned for identifying customer requirements?
- How have you identified the completeness, fitness for purpose, statutory, regulatory, and other obligations for the product?
- How have you planned for availability, delivery, and support of the product?

Continued on next page

7.2 Customer-Related Processes, Continued

7.2.2 Review of Product Requirements

Requirements

Your organization must review the identified customer requirements together with additional requirements determined by the organization.

The review must be conducted prior to committing to supply a product to the customer; for example, submission of a tender, acceptance of a contract, or order.

Record results of the review and subsequent follow-up actions.

Where product requirements are changed, you must ensure that relevant

- documentation is amended, and
- personnel are made aware of the changed requirements.

What this means

When reviewing product requirements

- define, implement, and maintain processes to ensure adequate understanding of the needs and expectations of customers, and
- include identification and review of relevant information in these processes.

Review customer requirements

Review the identified requirements, which can be done with customers and other interested parties.

This review needs to occur prior to committing to supply product, as described in a contract.

Continued on next page

7.2 Customer-Related Processes, Continued

7.2.2 Review of Product Requirements, Continued

Product requirements

Ensure that product requirements are

- defined
- confirmed before acceptance, and
- able to meet the requirements.

Required changes and records

Ensure that all reviews, changes, and follow-up actions to product requirements are

- amended in the appropriate documentation
- communicated to relevant personnel
- implemented through a process to control the changes, and
- recorded.

Evidence

The list of evidence required for this section of the Standard should demonstrate that the review of customer requirements

- contains defined product requirements, and other requirements determined by your organization
- is done prior to committing to supply product
- is confirmed before acceptance where there are non-written requirements
- contains resolution when there are differences between a quote and a contract and subsequent follow-up actions are recorded, and
- contains relevant amended documentation when product requirements are changed.

Note: Relevant personnel must be informed of the changes.

Continued on next page

7.2.2 Review of Product Requirements, Continued

Auditor questions   Typical questions that may be asked by an auditor include:

- How do you conduct the review of customer requirements?
- How do you confirm customer acceptance when there are no written requirements?
- Where are your records of review and subsequent follow-up actions?
- How do you ensure that relevant personnel are informed of changes when there are changes to the requirements?

Continued on next page

7.2 Customer-Related Processes, Continued

7.2.3 Customer Communication

Requirements

Your organization must identify and implement arrangements for communication with customers.

What this means

Implement effective liaisons with customers, with the aim of meeting customer requirements. Define how you will communicate regarding

- product information
- inquiries
- contracts or order handling
- amendments
- customer feedback, and
- customer complaints.

Evidence

The list of evidence required for this section of the Standard includes customer communication regarding

- product(s)
- inquiries
- contracts
- order handling, and
- customer feedback, including complaints.

Auditor questions

Typical questions that may be asked by an auditor include:

- What is your implemented process to communicate with customers?
- What is included in your communications with your customers?
- How do you include customer feedback and customer complaints in your process?

7.3 Design and Development

7.3.1 Design and Development Planning

Requirements   Your organization must not only plan the product, but it must
also control the design and development of the product.

Interfaces between different groups involved in design and
development must be managed to ensure effective communication and clarity of responsibilities.

Planning output must be updated, as appropriate, as the
design and development progress.

What this means   Plan a process for designing and developing products or
processes.

The ***design control process*** is usually in the form of a cycle
that

- ensures that interfaces between different functions involved
  have clear responsibility and effective communication
- allows for continual improvement through each cycle pass
- is driven at each stage by the needs of the customer, and
- provides feedback to the customer, as appropriate.

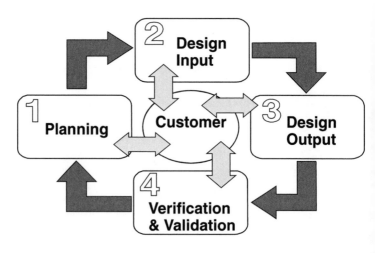

Continued on next page

7.3.1 Design and Development Planning, Continued

What this means (continued)	The information that follows provides the details of each stage.
Planning consideration	When designing or developing planning, consider life cycle, safety, dependability, durability, maintainability, ergonomics, the environment, disposal, and other risks.
Planning control	Plan for the control of the product during the different stages of design and development. To do this, determine the following: • design and development activity, and • review, verification, and validation activity. *Note*: During the planning, ensure responsibility and authority for those activities.
Interfaces	Ensure all the interested parties involved in the design and development communicate effectively and understand their responsibilities.
Planning output	Update the output of your planning as the design and development progresses.

Continued on next page

7.3 Design and Development, Continued

7.3.1 Design and Development Planning, Continued

Evidence

The list of evidence required for this section of the Standard includes design and development planning methodology that determines

- design and development stages
- review, verification, and validation appropriate to each stage
- responsibilities and authorities
- effective communication among all parties, and
- planning output updates as appropriate.

Auditor questions

Typical questions that may be asked by an auditor include:

- How do you plan for the control of the design and development of your product?
- What is included in the planning process of your product?
- How have you determined the responsibilities and authorities for each of the stages in your design and development?
- How do you manage the effective communication between all interested parties in the design and development?

Continued on next page

7.3 Design and Development, Continued

7.3.2 Design and Development Inputs

Requirements	Your organization needs to • define and document inputs relating to product • review the inputs for adequacy, and • resolve incomplete, ambiguous, or conflicting requirements.
What this means	Define and document the inputs that you use to meet the product requirements. These may include internal, external, and other inputs.
Required documentation	Document inputs relating to product requirements.

Example: Internal inputs	Examples of internal inputs include • policies • standards and specifications • skill requirements • dependability requirements, and • documentation and data on existing products.

Continued on next page

7.3.2 Design and Development Inputs, Continued

Example:
External inputs

Examples of external inputs include

- customer or marketplace needs and expectations
- contractual requirements
- relevant statutory/regulatory requirements
- international/national standards, and
- industry codes of practice.

Reviewing inputs

Review the requirement inputs for adequacy. Any incomplete, ambiguous, or conflicting requirements should be resolved.

Evidence

The list of evidence required for this section of the Standard includes

- defined and documented requirement inputs
- inputs that contain functional and performance requirements that have
  - applicable regulatory and statutory requirements, and
  - applicable information derived from previous similar designs
- any other requirements essential for design and development.

Auditor questions

Typical questions that may be asked by an auditor include:

- Where are the inputs for defined and documented requirements?
- How do you identify inputs for the product design and development?
- How do you review the inputs for adequacy?
- How do you resolve conflicting requirements?

Continued on next page

7.3 Design and Development, Continued

7.3.3 Design and Development Outputs

Requirements

Your organization must provide the outputs of the design and development process in a manner that enables verification against the design and development inputs.

Design and development outputs must be approved prior to release.

What this means

Provide the outputs from the design and development process. The outputs should lead to realization of the product and also include information necessary to satisfy the needs and expectations of customers and other interested parties.

Examples include

- product specifications
- training requirements
- purchasing requirements, and
- acceptance criteria.

Recommended documentation

The outputs of the design and development should be documented. They need to be documented in a manner that enables verification against the design and development inputs.

Continued on next page

7.3.3 Design and Development Outputs, Continued

Verification The outputs need to

- provide evidence that they meet the input requirements
- contain or reference acceptance criteria to evaluate the product, and
- define the characteristics of the product that are essential to its safe and proper use, such as training requirements.

Important The outputs need to be approved prior to release.

Evidence The list of evidence required for this section of the Standard includes

- documented outputs to enable verification
- comparison against design and development input requirements
- appropriate information for production and service operations
- references to product acceptance criteria
- characteristics of the product that are essential for safe and proper use, and
- approval prior to release.

Auditor questions Typical questions that may be asked by an auditor include:

- Where are the outputs of the design and development process documented?
- How do the outputs meet the design and development input requirements?
- Where are the acceptance criteria referenced?
- How are design and development outputs reviewed prior to release?

Continued on next page

7.3 Design and Development, Continued

7.3.4 Design and Development Review

Requirements   Your organization, at suitable stages, must conduct systematic reviews of design and development to

- evaluate the ability to fulfill requirements, and
- identify problems and propose follow-up actions.

Participants in such reviews must include representatives of functions concerned with the design and development stage(s) being reviewed.

You must record the results of reviews and subsequent follow-up actions.

What this means   Maintain reviews of the design and development to evaluate the ability to meet requirements, identify problems, and propose necessary actions.

Required record   Keep a record of the reviews and subsequent follow-up actions.

RECORD

Conduct reviews   Conduct periodic reviews to consider design and development objectives, including, as appropriate,

- meeting verification and validation goals
- evaluating potential hazards or modes of failures in product use
- following life cycle data on performance of the product, and
- reviewing potential impact of the product on the environment.

Continued on next page

7.3.4 Design and Development Review, Continued

Attendance at reviews

Representatives of functions concerned with the design and development stage(s) need to attend the reviews and propose follow-up actions to identified problems.

Evidence

The list of evidence required for this section of the Standard includes ensuring

- functional representation at reviews
- systematic reviews are done, and
- follow-up actions are recorded.

Auditor questions

Typical questions that may be asked by an auditor include:

- Who participates in design and development reviews?
- At what stage(s) are design and development reviews conducted?
- How do your records reflect the results of the reviews and the subsequent follow-up actions?

Continued on next page

7.3 Design and Development, Continued

7.3.5 Design and Development Verification

Requirements
Your organization must perform design and development verification to ensure the outputs meet the design and development inputs.

You must record the results of the verification and subsequent follow-up actions.

What this means
Verify that the outputs meet the design specification.

Required record
Keep a record of the verification and subsequent follow-up actions.

RECORD

Verification examples
Examples of verification activities include

- using comparative methodologies, such as alternative design and development calculations
- evaluating the activities against similar products, and
- testing, simulations, or trials to check compliance with specific input requirements.

Evidence

The list of the evidence required for this section of the Standard includes:

- design and development verification activities, and
- records of verification activities and subsequent follow-up actions.

Continued on next page

7.3 Design and Development, Continued

7.3.5 Design and Development Verification, Continued

Auditor questions Typical questions that may be asked by an auditor include:

- What are your verification activities?
- Where are your records of verification and subsequent follow-up actions?

Continued on next page

7.3 Design and Development, Continued

7.3.6 Design and Development Validation

Requirements Your organization must perform design and development validation to confirm that the resulting product is capable of meeting the requirements for intended use.

You need to record the results of the validation and subsequent follow-up actions.

What this means Ensure that the requirements for a specific intended use or application have been fulfilled.

Required record Keep a record of the results of the validation and subsequent follow-up actions.

RECORD

Partial validation When validation cannot occur, because it is impractical prior to the delivery or implementation of the product, partial validation may be necessary. This can be accomplished by reviewing

- engineering designs prior to construction, installation, or application
- software outputs prior to installation or use, and
- direct customer services prior to widespread introduction.

Evidence The list of evidence required for this section of the Standard should include validation records that confirm the resulting product met the requirements and was completed prior to delivery or implementation.

In addition, ensure, where it is impractical to complete a full validation, that a partial validation can be performed.

Continued on next page

7.3.6 Design and Development Validation, Continued

Auditor questions   Typical questions that may be asked by an auditor include:

- What design validation has been done?
- What is the process for validation?
- How are the results of the validation and subsequent follow-up actions recorded?

Continued on next page

7.3 Design and Development, Continued

7.3.7 Control of Design and Development Changes

Requirements	Your organization must identify, document, and control design and development changes, and verify, validate, and approve changes before implementation.

What this means Control of the design and development changes includes

- identifying, documenting, and controlling changes
- evaluating the effects of changes on the developing product, parts, and delivered product, and
- verifying, validating as appropriate, and approving before implementation.

Required documentation Document the results of the review of changes and subsequent follow-up actions.

Required record Record the results of the review of changes and subsequent follow-up actions.

Evaluating the changes Determine what the effects of the changes will be on parts and delivered products. Ensure that the design is still valid. Evaluate changes for their impact on all product characteristics.

Continued on next page

7.3 Design and Development, Continued

7.3.7 Control of Design and Development Changes, Continued

Verifying the changes	Re-verify the changes, as appropriate, to ensure that product specifications are fulfilled. Use methods such as testing, calculations, and prototypes.
Re-validating the changes	Re-validate changes, as appropriate, before implementation, and ensure that the change does not reduce the quality of the product.
Approving the changes	Approve all changes prior to release to ensure that customer needs are still being met.
Evidence	The list of evidence required for this section of the Standard includes • documented design and development changes • documented results of the review of changes and subsequent follow-up actions • evaluation of the effects of the changes on constituent parts and delivered products • verification of the changes • validation of the changes, and • approval of the changes.
Auditor questions	Typical questions that may be asked by an auditor include: • How do you evaluate the effects of changes on individual parts and delivered products? • How do you verify changes? • How do you validate changes? • How do you approve changes? • Do you have an approval cycle before implementation? • Where are your documented results on the review of changes and subsequent follow-up actions?

7.4 Purchasing

7.4.1 Purchasing Process

Requirements

Your organization must control its purchasing processes to ensure purchased product conforms to requirements. The type and extent of control must be dependent on the effects on subsequent realization processes and their output.

The results of evaluations and follow-up actions must be recorded.

What this means

Purchasing control involves

- having a purchasing process
- ensuring that the product you purchase conforms to specified requirements
- evaluating and selecting suppliers
- defining criteria for selection and periodic evaluation, and
- recording the results of evaluation(s) and follow-up actions.

Required process

Your organization needs to identify and implement purchasing processes for selection, evaluation, and control of purchased products to ensure they satisfy its needs and requirements.

Recommended documentation

It is recommended that you document the criteria for selection and periodic evaluation of suppliers.

Continued on next page

7.4.1 Purchasing Process, Continued

Required record Keep the results of evaluations of suppliers and follow-up actions.

What to include in purchasing control Purchasing processes should include

- identification of needs
- total cost of purchased product
- inquiries and price quotes
- ordering supplies
- verification of purchased products
- selection of suppliers
- purchase documentation
- nonconforming purchased products
- supplier control and supplier development, and
- assessment of risks associated with purchased product.

Supplier selection Evaluate and select suppliers based on their

- relevant experience
- response to problems
- potential capability to provide required product(s) efficiently and within schedule
- references for customer satisfaction
- service and support, and
- locations and resources.

Continued on next page

Evidence

The evidence required for this section of the Standard includes

- defining a process to control purchases
- purchasing product that conforms to requirements
- evaluating and selecting suppliers based on their ability to meet the organization's requirement(s)
- defining criteria for selection and periodic evaluation, and
- recording the results of evaluations and follow-up actions.

Auditor questions

Typical questions that may be asked by an auditor include:

- How do you ensure that purchased product conforms to requirements?
- How do you evaluate and select suppliers?
- Where are your criteria for selection and periodic evaluation defined?
- Where are the results of evaluations and follow-up actions recorded?

Continued on next page

7.4 Purchasing, Continued

7.4.2 Purchasing Information

Requirements

Your organization must contain information in its purchasing documents that describes the product to be purchased.

Your organization must ensure the adequacy of specified requirements contained in the purchasing documents prior to their release.

What this means

Ensuring purchasing orders means you must have enough information to describe the specified requirements.

Evidence

The evidence required for this section of the Standard shows that your purchasing documents contain

- requirements, where appropriate for approval or qualification of
  - product
  - procedures
  - processes
  - equipment, and
  - personnel, and
- Quality Management System requirements.

Also, have evidence to ensure the adequacy of the specified requirements prior to their release.

Auditor questions

Typical questions that may be asked by an auditor include:

- What information is contained in your purchasing documents?
- How do you ensure the adequacy of your specified requirements is contained in your purchasing documents?

Continued on next page

7.4 Purchasing, Continued

7.4.3 Verification of Purchased Product

Requirements

Your organization must identify and implement the activities necessary for verification of purchased product.

What this means

Determine and establish verification activities to ensure effective control of purchased product. Verification activities can be completed by your supplier, your organization, or a combination of both.

Evidence

The evidence required for this section of the Standard includes purchasing information that

- identifies and implements activities necessary for verification of purchased product
- specifies intended verification arrangements with your supplier when verification is performed at your supplier's site, and
- specifies the method of product release.

Auditor questions

Typical questions that may be asked by an auditor include:

- What are the verification activities for purchased product?
- Where have you implemented verification activities?
- Where have you specified verification arrangements when they are to be performed at a supplier's site?
- Where have you specified the method of product release from a supplier's site?

7.5 Production and Service Provision

7.5.1 Control of Production and Service Provision

Requirements	Your organization must control production and service operations.

What this means	Control your production and service operations by providing, as applicable,

- information that specifies the characteristics for the product
- work instructions
- suitable equipment
- availability and use of devices for measuring and monitoring production and service operations
- activities for monitoring and measuring these processes, and
- processes that address release, delivery, and applicable post-delivery activities.

Required process	Identification and definition of the processes for release, delivery, and applicable post-delivery activities are required in this section of the Standard. The required processes may include considerations for preservation and training.

Recommended documentation	Document the processes for release, delivery, and applicable post-delivery activities, and ensure that the information specifies the requirements before they are introduced into a process.

Work instructions	Document, where appropriate, work instructions to control how work is completed.

Continued on next page

7.5 Production and Service Provision, Continued

7.5.1 Control of Production and Service Provision, Continued

Device control activities

Ensure that you have

- suitable equipment that is properly maintained
- established measuring and monitoring devices to use for the proper maintenance of such equipment, and
- established and implemented monitoring activities, which can be paper-based or electronic.

Evidence

The evidence required for this section of the Standard includes

- demonstrated control over production and service operations
- work instructions, where necessary
- products and/or services that conform to specifications
- availability and use of measuring and monitoring devices, as appropriate, and
- defined processes for release, delivery, and applicable post-delivery activities.

Auditor questions

Typical questions that may be asked by an auditor include:

- What control do you put on your production and service operations?
- What information is available that shows the requirements of the product?
- What work instructions are available?
- What kinds of monitoring activities do you employ?
- What defined processes for release, delivery, and applicable post-delivery activities do you employ?

Continued on next page

7.5 Production and Service Provision, Continued

7.5.2 Validation of Processes

Requirements

Your organization must validate any production and service processes where resulting output cannot be verified by subsequent measurement or monitoring. This includes any processes where deficiencies may become apparent only after the product is in use or the service has been delivered.

Validation must demonstrate the ability of the process to achieve planned results.

What this means

Confirm that your production and service processes meet the product needs and expectations of customers when you cannot verify the product by monitoring activities.

Required processes

Establish and define validation processes that include, as appropriate,

- the approval of validation processes
- how equipment and personnel will be accepted
- what methodologies and procedures will be used
- what records will be required, and
- how you will re-validate the process.

Validation documentation and records

Documenting the arrangements for validation is recommended. Have a record of the validation if your process is defined, as applicable.

Continued on next page

7.5 Production and Service Provision, Continued

7.5.2 Validation of Processes, Continued

Product deficiencies

Deficiencies in the product sometimes do not occur until after the product is in use or the service has been delivered. Activities such as modeling, simulation, trials, and reviews involving customers or other interested parties may need to be completed.

Evidence

The evidence required for this section of the Standard includes a validation process when resulting product or service cannot be verified by measurement or monitoring.

The validation process should indicate that you

- achieved planned results
- approved the process(es), equipment, and personnel
- used defined methods and procedures
- had requirements for records, when applicable, and
- included re-validation, when applicable.

Auditor questions

Typical questions that may be asked by an auditor include:

- What is your validation process for product(s) or service(s) that cannot be verified by measurement or monitoring?
- How does validation demonstrate the ability of the process to achieve planned results?
- What are your requirements for validation records?

Continued on next page

7.5 Production and Service Provision, Continued

7.5.3 Identification and Traceability

Requirements

Your organization must:

- provide any necessary identification and traceability of product, and
- control and record the unique identification of the product, where traceability is a requirement.

What this means

Establish a process and documentation for identifying and tracing control of products to satisfy customer and other interested party requirements, if this is appropriate for your organization.

Rationale

The rationale for identification and traceability can be due to

- the status of products, including component parts
- contract requirements
- relevant statutory and regulatory requirements
- intended use of application
- use of hazardous materials, and
- risk mitigation.

Required records

Control and record the unique identification of the product where traceability is a requirement.

RECORD

Required process

Establish a process that shows how you identify and trace product(s).

Continued on next page

7.5 Production and Service Provision, Continued

7.5.3 Identification and Traceability, Continued

Evidence

The evidence required for this section of the Standard includes:

- a process to control and identify product(s)
- product identified throughout production and service operations
- measured and monitored product status, and
- records of product identification.

Auditor questions

Typical questions that may be asked by an auditor include:

- How have you determined that you need traceability for your product(s)?
- How do you uniquely identify product(s) throughout the production and service operations?
- How do you know a product's measurement and monitoring status?
- Where traceability is required, how is the unique identification of product controlled and recorded?

Continued on next page

7.5 Production and Service Provision, Continued

7.5.4 Customer Property

Requirements

Your organization must

- exercise care with customer property while it is under the organization's control, and
- identify, verify, protect, and maintain customer property provided for use or incorporation into the product.

What this means

You need to be responsible for customer property that is supplied to you by your customer and is under your control and/or is incorporated into the product.

Example: A customer supplies its corporate logo emblem for attachment to your product.

Required record

Record and report to the customer any customer property that is lost, damaged, or otherwise found to be unsuitable for use.

RECORD

Verify customer property

Demonstrate that your organization has the correct customer property and confirm that you are protecting and maintaining its value.

Continued on next page

7.5 Production and Service Provision, Continued

7.5.4 Customer Property, Continued

Evidence

The evidence required for this section of the Standard includes

- implementing a process that identifies, verifies, protects, and maintains customer property
- maintaining records of lost, damaged, or otherwise unsuitable-for-use customer property, and
- maintaining records of reports to customers when property has been lost, damaged, or otherwise made unsuitable for use.

Note: Customer property may include intellectual property.

Auditor questions

Typical questions that may be asked by an auditor include:

- Where are your records that are reported to the customer when customer property is lost, damaged, or otherwise made unsuitable for use?
- What is your process for identifying, verifying, protecting, and maintaining customer property?

Continued on next page

7.5 Production and Service Provision, Continued

7.5.5 Preservation of Product

Requirements

Your organization must preserve conformity of product with customer requirements during internal processing and final delivery to the destination. Product preservation must include identification, handling, packaging, storage, and protection.

What this means

Protect and prevent the product from damage, deterioration, or misuse during all internal processing and final delivery. To do this, consider the need for any special requirements arising from the nature of the product.

Special requirements may be associated with

- software
- electronic media
- hazardous materials
- specialist personnel, and
- products or materials that are unique or irreplaceable.

Preserving product

This table provides a list of activities and your requirements for preserving customer product and parts of customer product.

Activity	What to Ensure
Identification	Unique identification.
Handling	Proper control of the handling of the product and parts of the product.
Packaging	Appropriate packaging to ensure conformity in delivery.
Storage	Avoidance of deterioration.
Protection	Products and parts of a product protected from conditions that would not control conformity.

Continued on next page

7.5 Production and Service Provision, Continued

7.5.5 Preservation of Product, Continued

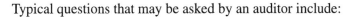

Evidence

The evidence required for this section of the Standard includes preservation to ensure conformity of the product by

- identifying
- handling
- packaging
- storing, and
- protecting the product and parts of the product.

Example: Implementation of a shelf-life program to prevent deterioration.

Auditor questions

Typical questions that may be asked by an auditor include:

- How do you ensure conformity of the product?
- How do you control the identification, handling, packaging, storage, and protection of the product and/or constituent parts of the product?
- How is the product handled to prevent damage?
- How does packaging provide for adequate protection of the product?

7.6 Control of Monitoring and Measuring Devices

Requirements

Your organization must identify the measurements to be made and the measuring and monitoring devices required to ensure

- conformity of the product to specified requirements, and
- measurement capability is consistent with measurement requirements.

What this means

Determine which measurements and test equipment you will use to ensure conformity of product.

Calibrating test equipment

Calibrate each item of test equipment against certified test equipment having a known valid relationship to nationally recognized standards, such as the National Institute of Standards and Technology (NIST).

Where no nationally recognized standard exists, the basis of the calibration must be recorded.

Required process

Establish a process to ensure that monitoring and measuring can be carried out.

Required record(s)

Record the results of the calibration and the basis for calibration when no international or national standards exist.

RECORD

Protecting the devices

Protect the monitoring and measuring devices from unauthorized adjustments, damage, and deterioration to maintain confidence in the results.

Continued on next page

7.6 Control of Monitoring and Measuring Devices, Continued

Validity of measuring results

When equipment is found not to conform to requirements at calibration, access and record the validity of previous measuring results.

Evidence

The evidence required for this section of the Standard includes determining

- which measurements to make
- which measuring and monitoring devices are required
- how to calibrate and adjust the devices
- how to safeguard and protect the devices, and
- what corrective action to take when test results indicate that equipment is out of calibration.

Ensure that you have recorded the

- results of the calibration
- basis of the calibration used when there were no national or international standards, and
- validity of the previous measuring results when equipment is found to be out of calibration.

Auditor questions

Typical questions that may be asked by an auditor include:

- How do you identify which measuring and monitoring devices you will select for the measurements to be made?
- How do you determine if devices are calibrated and adjusted?
- What evidence do you have to show that your calibration devices are traceable to a national or international standard(s)?
- How do you protect your devices from invalid adjustments, damage, or deterioration?
- What records do you maintain on the results of calibration?
- What is the process for corrective action when devices are found to be out of calibration?

Chapter 8

Measurement, Analysis, and Improvement Requirements

Overview

Introduction   This chapter describes how to measure, analyze, and improve the Quality Management System.

In this chapter   This chapter contains the following topics.

8.1 General

Requirements   Your organization must plan and implement the measurement
                       and monitoring activities used to ensure conformity to speci-
                       fied requirements and attain continual improvement.

What this means   The purpose of this section is to ensure control of your
                       Quality Management System and provide continual
                       improvement.

                       Determine, provide, and implement measuring and monitor-
                       ing processes, including the need for and use of statistical
                       techniques.

Definition   *Statistical techniques* are the collection, analysis, interpreta-
                       tion, and presentation of data to provide information for con-
                       tinual improvement.

                       Notes:

                       • Trend and data analysis should identify variations in your
                         activities.
                       • Data should be analyzed and turned into information.

**Defining and   Define and plan what you will
planning activities**

                       • implement for measuring and monitoring activities
                       • record, collect, analyze, and evaluate, and
                       • summarize from the data to provide information for control
                         and improvement.

**Examples of   Examples of measuring and monitoring activities include
activities**

                       • using customer satisfaction surveys
                       • collecting and evaluating reworked data, and
                       • conducting internal audits.

Continued on next page

8.1 General, Continued

Recommended documentation

Document the planning of the measurement and monitoring activities that you will use to achieve

- conformity of product
- effectiveness of the processes, and
- customer satisfaction.

Evidence

The evidence required for this section of the Standard should address

- measurement and monitoring activities, and
- statistical techniques and applicable methodologies.

Auditor questions

Typical questions that may be asked by an auditor include:

- How have you planned for measurement and monitoring activities so that they provide for control of your process(es)?
- How have you planned to achieve continual improvement?
- What methods do you use for data analysis?

8.2 Monitoring and Measurement

8.2.1 Customer Satisfaction

Requirements	Your organization must determine the methodologies for obtaining, monitoring, and using information on customer satisfaction, including customer perception. This should be done on an ongoing basis to measure the performance of your quality system.

What this means	Ensure your organization has a method(s) for getting customer satisfaction information on a continual basis. Use this information to improve your quality system.

Note: Customer satisfaction indicates how you have met the customer's needs and expectations from the customer's point of view. |

Examples	Your organization needs to determine methods to obtain customer-related information. Examples include

• customer surveys
• customer complaint records, and
• documented communication with customers. |

Evidence	The evidence required for this section of the Standard should address the:

• identification and implementation of customer satisfaction methodologies, and
• results of customer satisfaction measurements. |

Continued on next page

128

8.2 Monitoring and Measurement, Continued

8.2.1 Customer Satisfaction, Continued

Auditor questions   Typical questions that may be asked by an auditor include:

- How have you determined the method(s) you use to obtain customer satisfaction data, and how do you use this data to measure the performance of the Quality Management System?
- How do you proactively monitor customer satisfaction?
- What are the results of your customer satisfaction measurements?

Continued on next page

8.2.2 Internal Audit

Requirements   Your organization must perform internal audits to ensure the requirements of the Standard are addressed and that your Quality Management System has been effectively implemented.

What this means   Ensure you have an internal quality audit plan (internal auditing process) that provides input to management on the conformance and effectiveness of your Quality Management System. The output of this process will serve as input to a timely and effective corrective action process.

Important: Verify by follow-up activities that the implemented corrective action resulting from the internal audit is effective.

Required documentation   Documented procedure(s) should address

- audit scope
- frequency of schedule for audits
- methods of conducting the audit
- responsibilities for conducting the audit
- independence of auditors, and
- recorded and reported results of the audit to management.

Required record   Ensure you record the results of internal audits.

Continued on next page

8.2.2 Internal Audit, Continued

Internal audit process

This table describes a typical internal audit process.

Stage	Who Is Responsible?	Description
1	Quality System Management	Develops audit plan.
2	Quality System Management	Schedules audits on the basis of status and importance of the activity.
3	Auditor	Audits the processes, including the effectiveness of any previous corrective action.
4	Auditor	Submits audit report of the processes audited to management.
5	Quality System Management	Reviews noncompliances.
6	Quality System Management	Takes timely corrective action on noncompliance activities.

Evidence

The evidence required for this section of the Standard includes

- documented internal audit procedure(s) defining the audit program, and
- results of the internal audit(s).

Continued on next page

8.2 Monitoring and Measurement, Continued

8.2.2 Internal Audit, Continued

Auditor questions   Typical questions an auditor might ask include:

- What is the internal quality audit plan (internal quality audit process)?
- How many internal quality audits are scheduled and conducted?
- How do these audits check conformance to requirements and effectiveness?
- How are auditors qualified?
- How do you ensure that audits are conducted by personnel other than those who perform the activity being audited?
- How are audit results recorded and brought to the attention of personnel responsible for the area audited?
- What corrective action is taken on deficiencies found in the audit?
- How do auditors ensure that corrective action, as a result of prior audits, has been effective and has eliminated deficiencies?
- How are results of audit reports used in the management review?

Continued on next page

8.2 Monitoring and Measurement, Continued

8.2.3 Monitoring and Measuring of Processes

Requirements

Your organization must monitor and, where applicable, measure the Quality Management System processes to demonstrate planned results.

What this means

Identify the measurement methods and conduct measurements to evaluate how the quality system processes are performing.

Examples

Some example of measurements include

- internal audits
- cycle time activities
- cost reduction, and
- process variation measurements.

Required process

Ensure you have identified key processes to monitor and, where applicable, measure. Implement monitoring and measurement methods.

Evidence

The evidence required for this section of the Standard includes

- process monitoring and measurement
- explanations of how applicable measurements meet process requirements, and
- results of process measurements.

Auditor questions

Typical questions that may be asked by an auditor include:

- What methods do you use to measure and monitor your processes?
- What processes do you measure and monitor?
- How do you determine which processes to measure and monitor?
- How do you ensure that measurements confirm process control?

Continued on next page

8.2.4 Monitoring and Measuring of Product

Requirements   Your organization must monitor and measure the characteristics of the product at appropriate developmental stages to ensure that customer requirements for the product are met, provide evidence of conformity to the documented acceptance criteria, and record who is responsible for release of product.

All specified activities need to be satisfied before product release, unless approved by the customer.

What this means   Define, measure, monitor, and document the inspection and testing of your product during product development.

This needs to be done prior to release. All criteria need to be met, unless otherwise approved by the customer.

Required   Document the acceptance criteria and evidence of conformity.
document

Required record   Ensure you have a record that the authority responsible has released the product and that the product conforms to the requirements.

Continued on next page

134

8.2.4 Monitoring and Measuring of Product, Continued

Examples of records

Some examples of product measurement records include

- inspection and test paper reports, and/or
- electronic data.

Evidence

The evidence required for this section of the Standard includes

- product measurement and monitoring
- verification that product requirements have been met
- conformance of product to acceptance criteria, and
- record of product release by authority responsible for release through the records.

Auditor questions

Typical questions that may be asked by an auditor include:

- How do you measure your product for acceptance verification?
- How do you verify that product requirements are met?
- Where are your records on the release of product?
- Where is your acceptance criteria defined?

8.3 Control of Nonconforming Product

Requirements Your organization must identify and control nonconforming product and follow a documented procedure to ensure that nonconforming product is not used or delivered.

When nonconforming product is corrected, you must re-verify it to demonstrate conformity to the requirements.

When nonconforming product is detected after delivery or use, you must take appropriate action based on the impact or potential impact of the nonconformity.

What this means Ensure that you document the process to identify, review, and dispose of nonconforming product.

You must have a documented procedure for the control of nonconforming product that describes how you will ensure the nonconformity is corrected or otherwise controlled. It may be required that the nonconformity be reported for concession to the customer.

Required documentation Document a procedure that addresses the control of nonconforming product.

Continued on next page

Nonconforming product process

The table below shows the five stages of a typical nonconforming product process.

Stage	Team Activities
1 Identification	Identify nonconforming product.
2 Evaluation	Evaluate extent of nonconformance.
3 Segregation	Segregate nonconforming product, either physically or through marking.
4 Notification	Notify all affected parties.
5 Disposition	Dispose of nonconforming product through • rework to meet the specified requirements • acceptance by concession with or without repairs • re-grading for alternative applications, or • scrap. *Note*: Repaired or reworked product requires re-inspection.

Required record

Ensure you have a record of the nature of the nonconformance and subsequent actions taken, including concessions made.

RECORD

Continued on next page

8.3 Control of Nonconforming Product, Continued

Evidence

The evidence required for this section of the Standard includes

- documented procedures describing the activities you use to control nonconforming product
- implemented activities for the control of nonconforming product
- re-verified correction of nonconforming product
- actions taken when nonconforming product is delivered or used by the customer, and
- concession reports from the customer when applicable.

Auditor questions

Typical questions that may be asked by an auditor include:

- What is the process for ensuring that nonconforming product is prevented from unintended use or installation?
- How is nonconforming product identified?
- What is the process for releasing product under an authorized concession?
- How do you identify and control nonconforming product?
- What action do you take when nonconforming product is detected after delivery or use?

8.4 Analysis of Data

Requirements

Your organization must determine the suitability and effectiveness of your Quality Management System and identify improvements by collecting and analyzing data from measuring and monitoring activities.

What this means

Review the data that has been collected and analyze it to assess whether the Quality Management System is effective and can be improved.

This analysis should provide information on

- customer satisfaction
- conformance to product requirements
- features of the processes, product, and their trends, and
- suppliers.

Look at trends, processes, and products to identify problems and initiate effective preventive action.

Evidence

The evidence required for this section of the Standard includes

- collected and analyzed data
- identified opportunities for improvement
- data from various sources, such as data collected from measuring and monitoring activities, and
- data on customer satisfaction, conformance to customer requirements, characteristics of processes, product, and their trends, and suppliers.

Continued on next page

8.4 Analysis of Data, Continued

Auditor questions   Typical questions that may be asked by an auditor include:

- What is your process for collecting and analyzing data?
- How do you identify improvements that can be made to the Quality Management System?
- How do you analyze the data to identify trends, performance, and customer satisfaction?
- What sources of data do you use to assess performance of the Quality Management System?

3.5 Improvement

3.5.1 Continual Improvement

Requirements   Your organization must plan for and seek to continually improve the Quality Management System. You must have a continual improvement process in place.

This continual improvement process must involve the use of

- the Quality Policy
- the Quality Objectives
- audit results
- data analysis
- corrective action
- preventive action, and
- management review.

What this means   Continually seek to improve the effectiveness of the Quality Management System, ensuring that you identify and manage improvement activities.

Seek to enhance the effectiveness of the Quality Management System continually through

- planning
- establishing objectives
- measuring and monitoring activities
- analyzing data
- implementing solutions, and
- reviewing changes.

Required process   Ensure you have a process that plans all the activities for continual improvement.

Continued on next page

8.5 Improvement, Continued

8.5.1 Continual Improvement, Continued

Evidence

The evidence required for this section of the Standard includes ensuring that the Quality Management System is effective through the use of:

- Quality Policy
- Quality Objectives
- audit results
- data analysis
- corrective actions
- preventive actions, and
- management reviews.

Auditor questions

Typical questions that may be asked by an auditor include:

- How do you manage your process(es) for continual improvement?
- How do you decide what improvements to make to the Quality Management System?

Continued on next page

8.5 Improvement, Continued

8.5.2 Corrective Action

Requirements

Your organization must eliminate the cause of nonconformities by taking corrective action, as appropriate, and documenting corrective action procedures.

What this means

Ensure you have documented corrective action procedures in place so that the cause of nonconformity is eliminated to prevent recurrence.

Required documentation

A documented procedure is required that describes all the corrective action activities, including

- identifying nonconformities
- identifying customer complaints
- determining causes of nonconformities
- evaluating actions to prevent nonconformities
- determining and implementing corrective action
- recording results, and
- reviewing actions taken.

Required record

Ensure you record the results of corrective action(s) taken.

Continued on next page

8.5 Improvement, Continued

8.5.2 Corrective Action, Continued

Corrective action process

The table below shows the stages of a typical corrective action process.

Stage	Team Activities
1 Nonconfor- mance identification	Identify nonconformance through • receipt of customer complaint, or • report of product nonconformity.
2 Cause investigation	Investigate the cause of the nonconformity relating to product, process, or quality system.
3 Corrective action	Determine the corrective action needed to eliminate the cause of the nonconformity.
4 Control application	Apply controls to ensure corrective action is implemented and effective.

Evidence

The evidence required for this section of the Standard includes

• corrective action procedures, and
• implementation of corrective actions to
  • identify nonconformities
  • identify customer complaints
  • determine the cause of nonconformity
  • evaluate actions for corrective action
  • determine and implement corrective action
  • record results, and
  • review effectiveness of corrective action.

Continued on next page

8.5 Improvement, Continued

8.5.2 Corrective Action, Continued

Auditor questions   Typical questions that may be asked by an auditor include:

- What is your documented procedure for corrective action?
- How does your corrective action process include identification of the cause of nonconforming product and the action to prevent recurrence?
- How are corrective actions made?
- How are corrective actions checked for effectiveness?
- How are sources of information included in your corrective action process?
- Where is your record(s) of the results of corrective action?

Continued on next page

8.5 Improvement, Continued

8.5.3 Preventive Action

Requirements

Your organization must identify preventive actions to eliminate the causes of potential nonconformities, prevent occurrence, and document the procedures for preventive action as appropriate.

What this means

Ensure you have a preventive action process in place to detect and eliminate potential causes of nonconforming product before it occurs.

Required documentation

A documented procedure is required that describes all the activities in the preventive action process, including

- identifying potential nonconformities and their causes
- determining and implementing preventive actions
- recording results, and
- reviewing preventive actions taken.

Preventive action process

The table below shows the stages of a typical preventive action process.

Stage	Team Activities
1 Potential cause identification	Identify • processes that affect product quality • concessions • audit results • Quality Management System records • service reports, and • customer complaints.
2 Potential cause investigation	Investigate the potential cause(s) of nonconformities.

Continued on next page

8.5 Improvement, Continued

8.5.3 Preventive Action, Continued

Preventive action process
(continued)

Stage	Team Activities
3 Preventive action	Determine the preventive action needed to eliminate the potential cause of nonconformities.
4 Control application	• Review change with management • revise documents • train personnel • implement change, and • apply controls to ensure preventive action is implemented and effective.

Required record   Ensure you have a record of preventive action(s) taken.

RECORD

Evidence   The evidence required for this section of the Standard should include preventive action procedure implementation activities that

- identify potential nonconformities and their causes
- implement preventive actions needed
- record results, and
- review preventive actions.

Continued on next page

8.5 Improvement, Continued

8.5.3 Preventive Action, Continued

Auditor questions   Typical questions that may be asked by an auditor include:

- Where is your documented procedure for preventive action?
- How are potential nonconformities and their causes identified?
- How are preventive actions implemented?
- How are preventive actions checked for effectiveness?
- Where are your record(s) of the results of preventive action?

Chapter 9

Transition Planning for ISO 9001:2000

Overview

Introduction	ISO 9000:1994 certificates will expire on December 15, 2003.
	Organizations must thoroughly plan a transition to the ISO 9001:2000 Standard since there are significant changes to the Quality Management System.
	Based on your registrar's policy and schedule, some organizations may need to transition to ISO 9001:2000 before that date. To prepare for the new ISO 9001:2000 requirements, organizations need to plan for and implement their transition.
Purpose of Chapter 9	The purpose of this chapter is to assist organizations transitioning from the 1994 requirements to the ISO requirements in the 2000 version.
	By highlighting the ISO 9001:2000 Standard's key new points of emphasis, we hope to provide the reader with things to consider for planning and implementing their compliance efforts.
	Organizations should consider the implications of new points in their transition planning, particularly the points found in the following clauses
	• Documentation (4.2) • Management Responsibility (5.0) • Training (6.2.2), and • Auditing (8.2.2).
	These clauses are highlighted because their effective implementation is critical to a successful transition.

Continued on next page

Assumptions for transition planning

This chapter assumes that the reader is

- familiar with the ISO 9000:1994 version of the standard
- knowledgeable about Quality Management Systems, and
- part of an organization that is currently certified or in compliance with ISO 9001/9002:1994.

Note: If you are not familiar with the 1994 version of the Standard, refer to the book *Demystifying ISO 9000: Information Mapping's Guide to the ISO 9000 Standards* by Gerard W. Paradis and Fen Small, 1994.

Transition process

The process that an organization should follow when transitioning to the ISO 9001:2000 Standard is described in the following table.

Stage	Description
1	Re-define the role of top management.
2	Analyze current processes to find opportunities for improvement.
	Note: Process tables and process flowcharts are excellent analytical tools.
3	Identify those processes that must be created where none existed previously.
4	Implement and train personnel to meet new processes.
5	Audit the new process.
6	Improve new processes based on the audits.

Continued on next page

Contents   This chapter contains the following topics.

Transition Planning and Implementation Processes

Introduction   There are several areas in the ISO 9001:2000 Standard where top management is expected to lead their organization in implementing a process approach to the Quality Management System. This topic provides suggested planning and implementation processes that need to be considered when making the transition.

New point of emphasis   The Standard now requires a planned process approach to the Quality Management System.

Implication   The implication of this new point of emphasis is that transitioning from ISO 1994 to ISO 9001:2000 must include planning and implementation processes that continually improve the organization's ability to be in compliance with the requirements.

Suggested planning process   This table provides a suggested process for planning a transition to the ISO 9001:2000 requirements.

Stage	Description
1	Top management commits to lead the organization toward continual improvement and embraces ISO 9001:2000.
2	Top management • selects a transition team • designates a leader, and • actively participates with the team.
3	Top management ensures training of the transition team to understand ISO 9001:2000.
4	Top management determines and plans for appropriate resource allocation for implementing continual improvement programs.
5	Transition team leader develops a project timeline with assigned tasks, personnel, and due dates.

Continued on next page

Transition Planning and Implementation Processes, Continued

Suggested implementation process

This table provides a suggested process for the transition team to use when implementing the transition to the ISO 9001:2000 Standard.

Stage	Description
1	Analyze the current process to find opportunities for improvement. *Note*: Process tables and process flowcharts are excellent analytical tools.
2	Document the process changes and any new processes that are created.
3	Integrate the new and revised documents into the document control system.
4	Determine and provide training on changes for appropriate personnel.
5	Audit and implement any changes resulting from the audit.
6	Schedule a pre-audit or formal certification audit.

Note: The organization should contact its registrar to determine his/her transition policies and schedule.

Documentation Considerations

Introduction	This topic provides suggestions for the transition team to consider when designing a documentation response to the ISO 9001:2000 requirements.
New points of emphasis	The ISO 9001:2000 Standard reduces the amount of required documents.
Implication	The implication of this new point of emphasis suggests that it is imperative that each organization analyze their current level of documentation and determine what is needed to ensure effective

• transition planning
• operation of critical quality management processes, and
• control of processes during the transition.

Note: Organizations do not have to change the current document structure (levels or tiers). However, the new requirements must be incorporated into your Quality Management System. In some cases, a documentation matrix may be used to cross-reference the existing numbering scheme to the ISO 9001:2000 requirements. This also helps the auditors understand where the new requirements are addressed.

Of course, organizations can re-number to the new Standard if they wish. |
| **What to look for** | Organizations must pay special attention to the documentation implications of ISO 9001:2000, including

• Section 4 - Quality Management System
• Section 5 - Management Responsibility, and
• Section 7 - Product Realization. |

Continued on next page

Documentation Considerations, Continued

What to look for in current documentation

Organizations need to review the current status of their ISO documents against the ISO 9001:2000 documentation requirements and ensure they have

- adequately documented their Quality Management System
- identified and documented key processes
- determined and documented the sequence and interaction of key processes
- established the need for documentation during product realization planning, and
- documented a Quality Policy, Quality Manual, and procedures and records where required by the Standard.

Recommendation: Organizations should continue to implement a structured documentation, control process, development process, and numbering system.

Amount of documentation

The amount of documentation differs from one organization to another due to

- relative size of the company
- type of business activity
- complexity of processes, and
- competency of personnel.

Opportunity for document improvement

This is an excellent opportunity to evaluate and discard current ineffective documentation and replace it with documents that are accessible, easy to understand, and easy to implement.

Four Levels of Documentation

Introduction   ISO documentation can still be viewed as existing on four levels (1-4). This perception helps document creators and coordinators manage the various documents that are part of any organization's Quality Management System.

This document provides a detailed description of the levels.

Level 1   Level 1 is the Quality Manual. This serves as a documented introduction to your Quality Management System, usually to a reader who is not familiar with it. The Quality Manual contains

- management policy and objectives
- the scope of the Quality Management System
- documented processes/procedures or references to them
- a designation of primary responsibilities, and
- a description of the interaction between the processes of the Quality Management System.

The Quality Manual probably will also contain a brief description of your organization and its major products or services.

A Quality Manual is usually not very large. A typical Quality Manual might comprise 20 to 30 pages.

Level 2   Level 2 documents explain what happens and how processes work in your Quality Management System. Many organizations refer to documents in Level 2 as processes.

A typical Level 2 document might contain

- a description of the process activity
- a description of the process controls
- definitions of terms used in the process description
- process responsibilities, and
- a document trail to supporting Level 3 documents.

Continued on next page

Four Levels of Documentation, Continued

Level 3

Level 3 documents tell you how to carry out specific operations or tasks.

There are several types of Level 3 documents, including

- hands-on directions, such as instructions or checklists
- training for specific operations
- reference data like specifications, standards, and product lists
- formats for forms
- a document trail to any other supporting documents, and
- a document trail to supporting Level 4 documents.

Note: Many organizations refer to Level 3 documents as standard operating procedures (SOPs), test methods, operating instructions, or work instructions.

Level 4

Level 4 consists of completed forms and reports that provide evidence that the organization has complied with the specified requirement in the Standard.

Examples include

- customer survey results
- test results reports
- management review meeting minutes
- training records
- nonconformance reports, and
- inspection results.

Management Responsibility Considerations

Introduction	This document provides suggestions for top management to consider when designing a management responsibility response to the ISO 9001:2000 requirements.
New point of emphasis	Top management's leadership role is expanded in the new ISO 9001:2000 Standard.
Implication	There is an emphasis in the Standard that top management must be heavily involved in determining the methods, policies, and objectives that constitute an organization's approach to the Quality Management System's requirements.
Shift from quality assurance	ISO 9001:2000 implies a shift in responsibility of the Quality Management System from quality assurance departments to top management explicitly.
Eight Quality Management Principles	The eight Quality Management Principles (see Chapter 3, Quality Management Principles) focus on business excellence and place emphasis on customer satisfaction. These principles must be used by top management to lead the organization toward continual improvement.
Considerations	Top management needs to be involved in

- creating and implementing a Quality Policy
- providing necessary resources for Quality Management System implementation
- communicating to personnel their role in achieving the Quality Objectives
- evaluating how well the organization uses measurement and data analysis to provide information for the continual improvement of the Quality Management System
- understanding how customer needs and expectations are identified, and

Continued on next page

Considerations
(continued)

- creating and implementing Quality Objectives that are
  - measurable
  - established at relevant functions, and
  - support the Quality Policy.

Training Considerations

<table>
<tr><td>Introduction</td><td>This topic provides suggestions for the transition team to consider when designing a training response to the ISO 9001:2000 requirements.</td></tr>
</table>

New point of emphasis

The ISO 9001:2000 Standard requires that the organization determine the necessary competence for its personnel performing work affecting product quality and to ensure

- its personnel are aware of the relevance and importance of their activities, and
- how the personnel contribute to the achievement of the Quality Objectives.

Implication

The implication of the requirement is that training alone does not adequately fulfill the organization's needs. The difference with previous requirements is that as a result of training, personnel must now be able to demonstrate their competence through their actions and be the able to apply their knowledge and skills to meet the organization's Quality Objectives.

It is important that management and your entire organization receive the appropriate Quality Management System training.

Training emphasis

An organization's training programs must emphasize the importance of meeting Quality Objectives and customer needs and expectations.

Considerations

It is recommended that training be provided to your organization to ensure personnel competence. Personnel need to understand the

- scope of the Quality Management System
- Quality Objectives
- customer needs and expectations, and
- key Quality Management System processes.

Continued on next page

Training Considerations, Continued

Considerations
(continued)

- process and product/service measurement needs
- existing documents and associated records
- appropriate documentation requirements
- internal auditing process, and
- their own responsibilities.

Internal Auditing Considerations

Introduction	This topic provides suggestions for the transition team to consider when designing an internal auditing response to the ISO 9001:2000 requirements.
New point of emphasis	The ISO 9001:2000 Standard increases the roles and responsibilities of auditors.
Implication	The auditors need additional training in the new requirements and must be able to audit key organizational processes, taking a process-oriented approach.
Audit planning	Develop an audit plan that links key business processes in all related areas in the ISO 9001:2000 Standard.

Audit planning:

Develop an audit plan that links key business processes in all related areas in the ISO 9001:2000 Standard.

For example, when auditing for compliance with the requirement for Quality Objectives, look beyond the primary section (5.4.1, *Planning Quality Objectives*) and include other related sections that address the Quality Objectives, such as

- 4.2.1a Quality Management System
- 5.1c Management Commitment
- 5.3c Quality Policy
- 5.4.2a Quality Management
- 5.6.1 Responsibility, Authority, and Communication
- 6.2.2d Competence, Awareness, and Training
- 7.1 Product Realization, and
- 8.5.1 Continual Improvement.

Continued on next page

Internal audit process

This table describes a typical internal audit process.

Stage	Responsibility	Description
1	Audit Leader	Develops audit plan.
2	Audit Leader	Schedules audits based on status and importance of activity.
3	Auditor	Audits organization, including effectiveness of any previous corrective action.
4	Auditor or Audit Leader	Submits audit report to management of the area audited.
5	Management	Reviews noncompliances.
6	Management	Takes timely corrective action on noncompliances.

Considerations

Since one of the major changes in the ISO 9001:2000 Standard is to focus on the effectiveness of the key processes in the Quality Management System, it is imperative that the auditors consider

- including customer needs and expectations
- learning general knowledge of the key processes and product being audited
- gaining some minimal understanding of the basic techniques in process control
- being able to determine and measure the effectiveness of the controlled process
- using the assistance of a technical expert when they don't have the general knowledge to evaluate if the process is being controlled properly, and
- understanding the role of associated records and evidence documentation.

Index

A

analysis requirements. *See* measurement, analysis and improvement requirements

auditor questions

    competence, awareness, and training, 78

    continual improvement, 142

    corrective action, 145

    customer communication, 91

    customer focus, 52

    customer product realization requirements, 87

    customer property, 119

    customer satisfaction, 129

    data analysis, 140

    design and development changes, control of, 106

    design and development inputs, 96

    design and development outputs, 98

    design and development planning, 94

    design and development review, 100

    design and development validation, 104

    design and development verification, 102

    documents, control of, 45

    human resources, 76

    identification and traceability of product, 117

    infrastructure, 80

    internal audits, 132

    internal communication, 64

    management commitment, 51

    management representative, 62

    management review, 66

    measurement, analysis and improvement requirements, 127

    monitoring and measuring devices, control of, 123

    nonconforming product, control of, 138

    planning, 58

    preservation of product, 121

    preventive action, 147

    processes, monitoring and measuring of, 133

    product realization, planning of, 85

    production and service provision, 113

    products, monitoring and measuring of, 135

    provision of resources, 75

    purchasing information, 110

    purchasing process, 109

    Quality Manual, 42

    quality objectives, 56

    quality policy, 54

    records, control of, 48

    responsibility and authority, 60

    review input, 69

    review of product requirements, 90

    review output, 71

    validation of processes, 115

    verification of purchased product, 111

    work environment, 81

audits

    certification audit stage of certification, 7

    defined, 33

    first-party audit, 33

Continued on next page

Continued on next page

Continued on next page

Continued on next page

Continued on next page

Continued on next page

About the Authors

Gerard W. Paradis Gerard W. Paradis is Senior Consultant and Trainer for Information Mapping, Inc., a worldwide leader in helping organizations improving quality system documentation. He co-authored the first edition of *Demystifying ISO 9001* (Prentice Hall PTR).

John R. Trubiano John R. Trubiano holds the titles of Senior Management Consultant, RAB Certified Lead Author, IQA/IRCA Registered Lead Auditor, and American Society for Quality (ASQ) Certified QE. A senior member of ASQ, he has over thirty years of experience in Quality Assurance Engineering and Management.

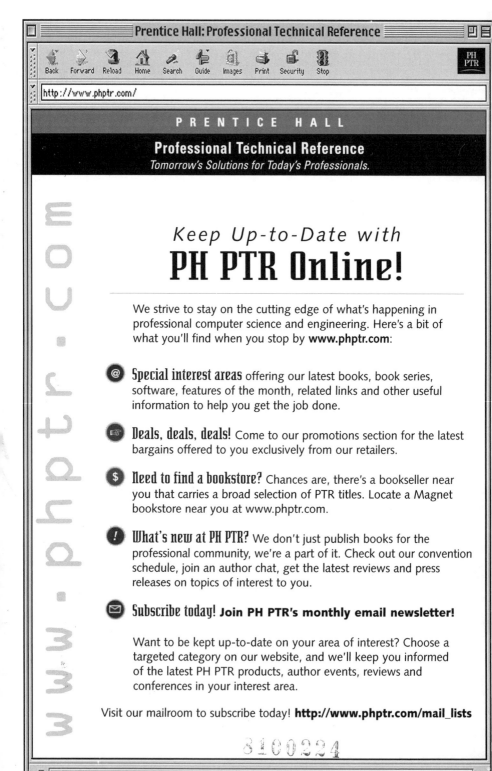

Prentice Hall: Professional Technical Reference

http://www.phptr.com/

PRENTICE HALL

Professional Technical Reference
Tomorrow's Solutions for Today's Professionals.

Keep Up-to-Date with
PH PTR Online!

We strive to stay on the cutting edge of what's happening in professional computer science and engineering. Here's a bit of what you'll find when you stop by **www.phptr.com**:

@ **Special interest areas** offering our latest books, book series, software, features of the month, related links and other useful information to help you get the job done.

Deals, deals, deals! Come to our promotions section for the latest bargains offered to you exclusively from our retailers.

$ **Need to find a bookstore?** Chances are, there's a bookseller near you that carries a broad selection of PTR titles. Locate a Magnet bookstore near you at www.phptr.com.

! **What's new at PH PTR?** We don't just publish books for the professional community, we're a part of it. Check out our convention schedule, join an author chat, get the latest reviews and press releases on topics of interest to you.

✉ **Subscribe today! Join PH PTR's monthly email newsletter!**

Want to be kept up-to-date on your area of interest? Choose a targeted category on our website, and we'll keep you informed of the latest PH PTR products, author events, reviews and conferences in your interest area.

Visit our mailroom to subscribe today! **http://www.phptr.com/mail_lists**

8100224